D0464679

ESSENTIALS OF
INVENTORY
MANAGEMENT

Second Edition

ESSENTIALS OF
INVENTORY
MANAGEMENT

Second Edition

Max Muller

WITHDRAWN
UTSA LIBRARIES

AMERICAN MANAGEMENT ASSOCIATION
New York · Atlanta · Brussels · Chicago · Mexico City
San Francisco · Shanghai · Tokyo · Toronto · Washington, D.C.

Bulk discounts available. For details visit:
www.amacombooks.org/go/specialsales
Or contact special sales:
Phone: 800-250-5308
E-mail: specialsls@amanet.org

View all the AMACOM titles at: www.amacombooks.org

This publication is designed to provide accurate and authoritative information in regard to the subject matter covered. It is sold with the understanding that the publisher is not engaged in rendering legal, accounting, or other professional service. If legal advice or other expert assistance is required, the services of a competent professional person should be sought.

Library of Congress Cataloging-in-Publication Data
Muller, Max
 Essentials of inventory management / Max Muller. -- 2nd ed.
    p. cm.
 Includes bibliographical references and index.
 ISBN-13: 978-0-8144-1655-6
 ISBN-10: 0-8144-1655-1
 1. Inventory control. I. Title.
 TS160.M83 2011
 658.7'87--dc22

                                                            2010039123

© 2011 Max Muller.
All rights reserved.
Printed in the United States of America.

This publication may not be reproduced, stored in a retrieval system, or transmitted in whole or in part, in any form or by any means, electronic, mechanical, photocopying, recording, or otherwise, without the prior written permission of AMACOM, a division of American Management Association, 1601 Broadway, New York, NY 10019

About AMA

American Management Association (www.amanet.org) is a world leader in talent development, advancing the skills of individuals to drive business success. Our mission is to support the goals of individuals and organizations through a complete range of products and services, including classroom and virtual seminars, webcasts, webinars, podcasts, conferences, corporate and government solutions, business books, and research. AMA's approach to improving performance combines experiential learning—learning through doing—with opportunities for ongoing professional growth at every step of one's career journey.

Printing Number

10   9   8   7   6   5   4   3   2   1

Library
University of Texas
at San Antonio

CONTENTS

Introduction to the Second Edition

When I wrote the first edition of *Essentials of Inventory Management* my objective was to present, in accessible language supported by copious illustrations and examples, timeless inventory management concepts and techniques. My purpose was to give the reader a fundamental understanding of inventory as it exists in the physical world (shelf count), and as an intangible item (record count) existing in a computer database and/or on paper.

The basic principles covered in that edition are as relevant today, even with the explosion of Internet-based e-commerce solutions to many inventory and materials management issues, as when they were first written.

I am pleased to note that the book was successful. It has been translated into Spanish, with distribution in a number of Spanish-speaking countries, and, an English-language soft cover edition is being distributed in India, Pakistan, Sri Lanka, Nepal, and Bangladesh. AMACOM Books and I have received excellent responses to the first edition from individuals just beginning their careers in fields related to inventory management, as well as from experienced materials managers who reported that the book reminded them of effective techniques they had known but had forgotten over the years.

Over the past several years, as I have continued to lecture and consult, it became apparent that the book could be enhanced by adding chapters and sections on subjects such as cycle counting, enterprise resource planning, and supply chain management. And so, this second edition was born.

The second edition retains the timeless, essential inventory management basics that are the hallmarks of the first edition, with new and expanded information that includes:

▸ An expansion of Chapter 2, "Inventory as Money," to include a section dealing with profit margins and merchandising metrics and containing both examples and formulae related to merchandising.

▸ A renamed Chapter 4, "Automated Inventory Identification Systems," with new material on Radio Frequency Identification Systems (RFID) that discusses the strengths and challenges associated with this technology.

▸ New coverage in Chapter 5, "Planning and Replenishment Concepts," of the benefits of enterprise resource planning (ERP), including the five main reasons why an enterprise should consider incorporating this concept into its organization.

▸ A revised and expanded Chapter 6, "Why Inventory Systems Fail and How to Fix Them," which includes new material regarding how to distinguish A-B-C cycle counting analysis using a single factor from approaches combining multiple factors (e.g., dollar value and usage rate). The chapter now explains in detail how to undertake an A-B-C cycle counting analysis by combining multiple factors.

▸ A new Chapter 7, "Basics of Supply Chain Risk Management," reveals how the very techniques that have allowed American businesses to slash operating costs and inventories by embracing just-in-time and lean manufacturing techniques have made them vulnerable to a number of serious supply chain risks. It offers suggestions regarding steps organizations should take in trying to balance the risks and rewards of SCM, and provides a starting point to any supply chain risk management effort.

And, of course, as it has since the first edition, the book introduces the new stockroom/warehouse manager, the nonfinancial inventory control individual, and the small business owner to the fundamental nature of inventory from financial, physical, forecasting, and operational standpoints. In addition, it explains in easily understandable terms the concepts underlying automated identification of product through both bar coding and RFID.

The ultimate goal of this book is to present immediately usable information in the areas of forecasting, physical control and layout, problem recognition, and resolution, as well as how to begin to better manage a supply chain.

Ultimately, *Essentials of Inventory Management* will enable you to:

▶ Understand that modern practice discourages holding large quantities of inventory and encourages only having amounts on hand required for current needs.

▶ Grasp the significance of controlling actual, on-hand inventory as both a physical object (shelf count) and as an intangible object (record count and monetary worth).

▶ Appreciate the fundamental differences between finished goods inventories in the retail/distribution sectors and raw materials and work-in-process inventories found in the manufacturing environment.

▶ Apply basic formulae to calculating inventory quantities.

▶ Utilize basic formulae to compute breakeven points, profit margins, markups and markdowns, as well as selling price and margin percentages.

▶ Select the cycle counting inventory method that is right for you.

▶ Undertake an A-B-C cycle counting analysis by combining multiple factors.

▶ Recognize and analyze dysfunctions within your own operation.

▶ Employ basic problem-solving techniques to issue resolution.

▶ Control the physical location of inventory in a more efficient manner.

▶ Analyze whether or not RFID is right for your organization.

▶ Be aware of supply chain management risks and possible solutions.

CHAPTER 1

INVENTORY AS BOTH A TANGIBLE AND AN INTANGIBLE OBJECT

The objective of this chapter is to provide you with a basic understanding of the nature of inventory as both a tangible, physical item actually kept within the facility ("real life" or "shelf count") and as an intangible item existing within the company's records ("paper life" or "record count"). Since you frequently make purchasing, sales, customer service, production planning, and other decisions based on whether an item is shown as being in-house as *per your records*, an item's paper life can be just as important as its real life.

Inventory—Who Needs It?

All organizations keep inventory. "Inventory" includes a company's raw materials, work in process, supplies used in operations, and finished goods.

Inventory can be as simple as a bottle of glass cleaner used as part of a building's custodial program or as complex as a mix of raw materials and subassemblies used as part of a manufacturing process.

INVENTORY COSTS

Inventory brings with it a number of costs, including:

- ▶ Dollars
- ▶ Space
- ▶ Labor to receive, check quality, put away, retrieve, select, pack, ship, and account for the item(s)
- ▶ Deterioration, damage, and obsolescence
- ▶ Theft

Inventory costs generally fall into ordering costs and holding costs. Ordering, or acquisition, costs come about regardless of the actual value of the goods. These costs include the salaries of those purchasing the product, costs of expediting the inventory, and so on. For a complete discussion of ordering costs, see Chapter 5, Planning and Replenishment Concepts. For a complete discussion of carrying costs, see Chapter 2, Inventory as Money.

As discussed in Chapter 2, holding costs include the cost of capital tied up in inventory (the opportunity cost of money[1]); storage costs such as rent; and costs of handling the product such as equipment, warehouse and stock-keeping staff, stock losses/wastage, taxes, and so on.

As discussed in Chapter 5, acquisition/ordering costs come about regardless of the actual value of the goods. These costs include the salaries of those purchasing the product, costs of expediting the inventory, and so on.

THE PURPOSE OF INVENTORY

So why do you need inventory? In a just-in-time manufacturing environment, inventory is considered waste. However, in environments where an organization suffers from poor cash flow or lacks strong control over (1) electronic information transfer among all departments and all significant suppliers, (2) lead times, and (3) quality of materials received, inventory plays important roles. Some of the more important reasons for obtaining and holding inventory are:

▸ *Predictability*: To engage in capacity planning and production scheduling, you need to control how much raw material and how many parts and subassemblies you process at a given time. Inventory buffers what you need from what you process.

▸ *Fluctuations in demand*: A supply of inventory on hand is protection. You don't always know how much you are likely to need at any given time, but you still need to satisfy customer or production demand on time. If you can see how customers are acting in the supply chain, surprises in fluctuations in demand are held to a minimum.

▸ *Unreliability of supply*: Inventory protects you from unreliable suppliers or when an item is scarce and a steady supply is difficult to ensure. Whenever possible, unreliable suppliers should be rehabilitated through discussions or replaced. Rehabilitation can be accomplished through master purchase orders with timed product releases, price or term penalties for nonperformance, better verbal and electronic communications between the parties, and so on. This will lower your on-hand inventory needs.

▸ *Price protection*: Buying quantities of inventory at appropriate times helps avoid the impact of cost inflation. Note that contracting to assure a price does not require actually taking delivery at the time of purchase. Many suppliers prefer to deliver periodically rather than to ship an entire year's supply of a particular stock keeping unit (SKU) at one time. (Note: The acronym "SKU" is a common term in the inventory world. It generally stands for a specific numeric or alpha-numeric identifier for a specific item.)

▸ *Quantity discounts*: Often bulk discounts are available if you buy in large rather than in small quantities.

▸ *Lower ordering costs*: If you buy a larger quantity of an item less frequently, the ordering costs are less than buying smaller quantities over and over again. (The costs of holding the item for a longer period of time, however, will be greater.) See Chapter 5, Planning and Replenishment Concepts. To hold down ordering costs and to lock in favorable pricing, many organizations issue blanket purchase orders coupled with periodic release and receiving dates of the SKUs.

TYPES OF STOCK

Inventory is basically divided into raw materials, finished goods, and work-in-process. Remember:

▸ *Raw materials*: Used to produce partial products or completed goods.

▸ *Finished product*: This is product ready for current customer sales. It can also be used to buffer manufacturing from predictable or unpredictable market demand. In other words, a manufacturing company can make up a supply of toys during the year for predictably higher sales during the holiday season.

▸ *Work-in-process (WIP)*: Items are considered to be WIP during the time raw material is being converted into partial product, subassemblies, and finished product. WIP should be kept to a minimum. WIP occurs because of such things as work delays, long movement times between operations, and queuing bottlenecks.

Other categories of inventory should be considered from a functional standpoint:

▶ *Consumables*: Light bulbs, hand towels, computer and photocopying paper, brochures, tape, envelopes, cleaning materials, lubricants, fertilizer, paint, dunnage (packing materials), and so on are used in many operations. These are often treated like raw materials.

▶ *Service, repair, replacement, and spare items (S&R items)*: These are after-market items used to "keep things going." As long as a machine or device of some type is being used (in the market) and will need service and repair in the future, it will never be obsolete. S&R items should not be treated like finished goods for purposes of forecasting the quantity level of your normal stock.

▶ Quantity levels of S&R items will be based on such considerations as preventive maintenance schedules, predicted failure rates, and dates of various items of equipment. For example, if an organization replaced its fluorescent tubes on an as-needed, on-failure basis, it would need a larger supply of these lights on hand at all times. However, if the same company relamped all of its ballasts once a year, it would buy a large quantity of tubes at one time and only keep a small supply on hand on an ongoing basis.

▶ Because S&R items are never "obsolete" or "dead" until the equipment or device they are to be used for is no longer in service, these items should not be included in calculating dead stock levels. See Chapter 2.

▶ *Buffer/safety inventory.* This type of inventory can serve various purposes, such as:

- Compensating for demand and supply uncertainties.
- "Decoupling" and separating different parts of your operation so that they can function independently from one another. See Exhibit 1–1.

▶ *Anticipation Stock.* This is inventory produced in anticipation of an upcoming season, such as fancy chocolates for Mother's Day or Valentine's Day. Failure to sell in the anticipated period could be disastrous, because you may be left with considerable amounts of stock past its perceived shelf life.

▶ *Transit inventory.* This is inventory en route from one place to another. It could be argued that product moving within a facility is transit inventory, but the common meaning refers to items moving within the distribution channel toward you, items outside of your facility, or items en route from your facility to the customer.

Transit stock highlights the need to understand not only how inventory physically moves through your system, but also how and when it shows up in your records. If, for example, 500 widgets appeared as part of existing stock while they were still en route to you, your record count would include them, but your shelf count would be 500 widgets short.

How could stock show up as part of inventory before it actually arrives? The answer depends on when title to the widgets transferred to you. Did title transfer when the product left the shipper's dock, or did it transfer only after the items arrived at your site and

Exhibit 1–1   Points Along the Channel of Distribution Where Buffer Stock Is Needed to Decouple Operations

→

Suppliers	Allows Procurement time to prepare purchase orders, place orders, and control timing and modes of delivery. Protects against uncertainties in lead times.	**Procurement (purchasing)**
Procurement (purchasing)	Provides time to plan and produce items while Procurement is interacting with Suppliers. Prevents downtime and allows for a continuous flow.	**Production**
Production	Provides Marketing with product to sell while Production is producing items for future sale.	**Marketing**
Marketing	Provides Distribution with the product Marketing has sold. Immediate customer satisfaction.	**Distribution**
Distribution	Offers the Intermediary items to deliver to the Consumer/End User.	**Intermediary (e.g., UPS, truck line, rail line, etc.)**
Intermediary (e.g., UPS, truck line, rail line, etc.)	Satisfies the Consumer/End User with product while it is waiting for deliveries from the Intermediary.	**Consumer/ End User**

were signed for? If title transferred when the product left the shipper's dock, it was then counted as part of your total inventory. As a result, your total record count would not match your shelf count. For example, if (a) a stockkeeper did not understand that an item's paper life had floated ahead of its real life and (b) the stockkeeper did not have a breakdown of items on hand, on order, in transit, and immediately available, (c) the stockkeeper would find a mismatch between the shelf and record counts. Inappropriate adjustments might then be made.

The Uniform Commercial Code (UCC) governs the transfer of title to product. The UCC has been adopted by most states. Article 2 of the UCC covers the sale of goods.

Tracking the Paper Life

To gain an understanding of the relationship between an item's real life and its paper life, follow a single item on its path through your system. In other words, track an item's physical movement through your facility while noting what is happening to its paper life during that same time period. You will be able to discover when one of these lives moves ahead of the other and when there are system errors, such as an item is moved but no paperwork exists authorizing that action.

Exhibit 1–2 provides an example of what could happen if an item's paper life and real life begin to leapfrog ahead or behind one another without the stockkeeper understanding the process.

As can be seen in Exhibit 1–2, an item's real life and paper life can leapfrog around one another. It is important to understand that these lives can exist independently of one another. To comprehend your own system, you must trace how both product and information move through the system. See Exhibit 1–3 for a simple

(text continues on page 13)

Exhibit 1–2 Real Life and Paper Life Leap Frog

Carr Enterprises operates six days per week, Monday through Saturday. It has an inventory system that is updated at 4:45 P.M. every day. In spite of the daily updating, the record count and the shelf count in Small Stock Room #1 are often out of balance.

Carr's warehouse manager, Nate, has decided to count everything in Small Stock Room #1 every Friday. He does so for two months. At the end of that time he is angry—the numbers still don't match.

Carr hires Shawn, an ace inventory detective, to help track down the source of the problem. Nate is flabbergasted. He believes he is counting very carefully, and if there is a problem, it is with the computer. Nate declares to anyone who will listen that "the computer is always wrong."

On Monday at 5:15 P.M., Shawn suggests that they examine an item that seems to be out of balance from the previous week's count.

Nate declares, "I'll show you one." Thrusting a brand new inventory Stock Status Report in front of Shawn's nose, Nate states, "Look at these widgets. It says there are 12 of them in stock. When we counted them last week there were 12 of them. I looked at this report this morning, and it said there were 13 of them. Now it says there are 12 of them, but I just looked in the stock room and there are actually 15 of them. See, I told you—the computer's always wrong."

Shawn asks if he can see Nate's count sheet with the widgets on it from the previous week. The sheet looks like this:

(continues)

(Exhibit 1–2 Continued.)

Stock Status Report					
Location	Part Number	Description	U/M	Quantity	
AB1002	9063	Gidgets	ea	127	
AB1003	2164	Gadgets	ctn	36	
AB1004	1878	Widgets	ea	~~18~~	12
AB1005	9201	Doodads	dz	98	
AB1006	5769	Whoohahs	pkg	~~105~~	101

Shawn asks what the notations mean.

Nate replies that when the wrong quantity was on the count sheet, he would "X" it out, write in the correct quantity, and turn the sheet into data entry.

Shawn asked when Nate turned his sheets in. Nate replied, "Friday—why?"

Shawn said, "I understand that you turn the sheets in on Friday. I'm asking, what time do you turn them in?" Nate says he does it at about 5 P.M. Thinking Shawn is criticizing him, Nate defensively states, "Hey, they're busy in data entry from 4:30 or so. They're doing cutoff and updates and stuff like that. So I wait until they're done."

Shawn asks when Nate's count sheets are keyed into the system. Nate says he doesn't know. Shawn asks Hillary, the data entry clerk, when Nate's sheets are keyed in. Hillary replies that she doesn't put Nate's work on the front burner, "if you know what I mean." Shawn persists. He asks again, "Who keys Nate's count sheets in and when are they done?" Hillary replies that she works on Saturday but leaves the sheets for Carolyn, the other data entry clerk, to input on Monday.

Shawn asks Hillary if she entered any widgets into the system on Saturday. She says she entered three of them into the system on Saturday. Shawn asks Carolyn how she handles inputting

Nate's information. She replies that she pulls up the item on her computer screen, checks to see if the total in the computer matches Nate's handwritten amount, and if it doesn't, she changes the amount in the system to match Nate's number.

Shawn charts-out the flow of real life and paper life for the widgets, and he comes up with the following:

Day	Record Count	Shelf Count	Notes
Friday @ close of business	10	12	At the start of business on Friday, the system believes there are 10 widgets. There are actually 12. Nate does not note a plus or minus amount on his count sheet. He X's through the 10 and writes in 12. He does not turn in his count sheets until after the system has been updated for that day. At the close of business on Friday, the system still believes there are 10 widgets. There are actually 12.
Saturday @ close of business	13	15	No one enters Nate's information on Saturday. Nate does not know this—he hasn't checked. Three widgets are added into the system on Saturday. At the close of business on Saturday, the system believes there are 13 widgets in stock. There are actually 15.
Monday morning	13	15	Monday morning's Stock Status Report reflects Saturday's numbers. During the day on Monday, Carolyn wipes out the record of 13 and enters the quantity of 12 from Nate's sheets.
Monday @ close of business	12	15	When the system is updated at 4:45 P.M. on Monday, the stock record and new Stock Status Report reflects that there are 12 widgets. There are actually 15. When Nate began counting on Friday the system was off by 2, and when all was said and done, it was off by 3![2]

(Exhibit 1–2 Continued.)

Exhibit 1–3 Tracking the Paper Life

Instructions: At each stage of the flow chart below note:

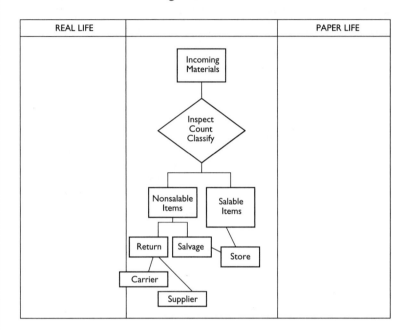

1. Where is the item physically?
2. What pieces of paper(s) authorize that?
3. When is information entered into your computer system?

   4. Who is supposed to write something down? What are they supposed to write down? When were they supposed to write it down? Who are they supposed to give the piece of paper to? What is that person supposed to do with it? When are they supposed to pass the piece of paper along?

   5. Does any item change its unit of measure within the system even though it retains the same physical form. For example: Item X is purchased by the master case. When it is entered into the database, a conversion table converts each case

into the four cartons within the master case. However, for ease of handling, the cartons remain in the master case for storage. Visually this item appears as a single unit while it will be sold or used as four separate items.

6. After the paper chase, where is the item physically?

method of breaking down a portion of your system to gain an understanding of your physical item and database float times.

Electronic Data Interchange

Stockkeepers who do not understand how and when an item's paper life is first created within a system become even more confused if there is no hard paper copy audit trail they can follow. How could:

▶ An order be placed?

▶ An order be accepted?

▶ Confirmation of the order be given?

▶ Shipping instructions be given?

▶ Notice of shipping arrangements be given?

▶ A paper life be created for an item in advance of it entering the facility?

All occur without any hard paper copies of these transactions. All of these events and others can occur in a paperless environment through electronic data interchange.

Electronic data interchange (EDI) is where routine business transactions are sent over standard communication lines (such as telephone lines) between computers within a company or between your computer and that of a vendor.

An example of EDI within a company occurs at the time of order entry, when information about that order is electronically transmitted to shipping or operations for order selection and shipping, to accounting for billing purposes, to sales for order verification, and so on.

An example of EDI with a vendor occurs when you electronically place an order directly from your computer into the vendor's computer. The vendor's computer then electronically confirms the order and transmits information about the order to the vendor's shipping and accounting departments. The vendor's computer also electronically notifies a carrier of the upcoming shipment. The carrier's computer electronically confirms the pickup and provides the vendor with pickup and delivery information. The vendor's computer then notifies your computer of the date, time, etc., of the upcoming delivery. All of this is accomplished without any human intervention other than the original placement of the order.

For EDI to work, all of the system participants must agree to strict rules regarding message content, format, and structure.

Recap

The objective of this chapter was to point out that inventory exists within your system as both a physical item and as an item in your records.

There are many reasons for obtaining and holding inventory, and inventory can play a variety of roles within the life of any organization.

To control and manage the items coming into, through, and out of your facility, it is important to understand not only where an item is physically located at any given time, but also how that existence is being acknowledged within the system.

REVIEW QUESTIONS

1. Inventory costs generally fall into:

   (a) sales expenditures.

   (b) work in process.

   (c) line during the annual physical inventory.

   (d) ordering costs and holding costs.

2. True or False

   EDI is when routine business transactions are sent over standard communication lines.

   (a) True

   (b) False

3. True or False

   Service and repair stock must never be retained beyond 5 years from date of purchase.

   (a) True

   (b) False

4. True or False

   Anticipation stock is inventory en route from one place to another.

   (a) True

   (b) False

5. Which Article of the Uniform Commercial Code governs the sale of goods?

   (a) 9

   (b) 1

   (c) 2

   (d) 117

Answers

1. (d), 2. (a), 3. (b), 4. (b), 5. (c)

Notes

1. If you have $2 million tied up in inventory, you cannot earn money (interest) on that money. If you could earn 10 percent interest on that $2 million, you could earn $200,000. Not being able to earn this money is an opportunity cost.

2. If you are going to note stock quantity changes but the information will not be input before there are intervening inventory events, you must use a "plus/minus" notation system (e.g., +3; −4; ±0). By using a plus/minus notation system, the data entry clerk will add or subtract from the then current amount, which will already include any intervening events.

CHAPTER 2

INVENTORY AS MONEY

Why should you care about the financial aspects of inventory? Because inventory is money.

Even if you do not have a financial background, it is important to understand and appreciate that inventory information in financial statements can be useful in the operation of your business. A basic understanding of how inventory appears on the balance sheet and its impact on the income statement and cash flow statement will improve your ability to have the right item in the right quantity in the right place at the right time.

Accounting for Inventories

The three basic types of inventory are:

1. Raw Materials—*raw materials inventory* is made up of goods that will be used in the production of finished products (e.g., nuts, bolts, flour, sugar).

2. Work in Process—*work in process inventory*, or *WIP*, consists of materials entered into the production process but not yet completed (e.g., subassemblies).

3. Finished Goods—*finished goods inventory* includes completed products waiting to be sold (e.g., bar stools, bread, cookies).

Most inventory fits into one of these general buckets, yet the amount of each category varies greatly depending on the specifics of your industry and business. For example, the types of inventory found in distribution environments are fundamentally different from those found in manufacturing environments. Distribution businesses tend to carry mostly finished goods for resale, while manufacturing companies tend to have less finished goods and more raw materials and work in progress. Given these differences, it is natural that the accounting choices vary between distribution and manufacturing settings.

How Inventory Is Valued

To assign a cost value to inventory, you must make some assumptions about the inventory on hand. Under federal income tax laws, a company can only make these assumptions once per fiscal year. Tax treatment is often an organization's chief concern regarding inventory valuation. The five common inventory valuation methods are as follows:

1. *First-in, First-out (FIFO)* inventory valuation assumes that the first goods purchased are the first to be used or sold regardless of the actual timing of their use or sale. This method is most closely tied to actual physical flow of goods in inventory. See Exhibit 2–1.

2. *Last-in, First-out (LIFO)* inventory valuation assumes that the most recently purchased/acquired goods are the first to be used or sold regardless of the actual timing of their use or sale. Since items you have just bought often cost more than those pur-

chased in the past, this method best matches current costs with current revenues. See Exhibit 2–1.

3. *Average Cost Method* of inventory valuation identifies the value of inventory and cost of goods sold by calculating an average unit cost for all goods available for sale during a given period of time. This valuation method assumes that ending inventory consists of all goods available for sale. See Exhibit 2–2.

Average Cost = Total Cost of Goods ÷ Total Quantity of Goods
Available for Sale   Available for Sale

4. *Specific Cost Method* (also *Actual Cost Method*) of inventory valuation assumes that the organization can track the actual cost of an item into, through, and out of the facility. That ability allows you to charge the actual cost of a given item to production or sales. Specific costing is generally used only by companies with sophisticated computer systems or reserved for high-value items, such as artwork or custom-made items.

5. *Standard Cost Method* of inventory valuation is often used by manufacturing companies to give all of their departments a uniform value for an item throughout a given year. This method is a "best guess" approach based on known costs and expenses, such as historical costs and any anticipated changes coming up in the foreseeable future. It is not used to calculate actual net profit or for income tax purposes. Rather, it is a working tool more than a formal accounting approach.

Inventory on the Balance Sheet

The balance sheet shows the financial position of a company on a specific date. It provides details for the basic accounting equation: Assets = Liabilities + Equity. In other words, assets are a company's

(text continues on page 22)

Exhibit 2–1 FIFO vs. LIFO vs. Average Cost Method of Inventory Valuation Example

Assume the following inventory events:

- November 5   Purchased 800 widgets at $10.00/unit
  —Total cost $8,000

- November 7   Purchased 300 widgets at $11.00/unit
  —Total cost $3,300

- November 8   Purchased 320 widgets at $12.25/unit
  —Total cost $3,920

- November 10   Sold 750 units of goods at $15.00/unit

- November 14   Sold 460 units of goods at $15.55/unit

- November 15   Purchased 200 widgets at $14.70/unit
  —Total cost $2,940

- November 18   Sold 220 units of goods at $14.45/unit

Basic Events:

UNITS PURCHASED			
Date	# Units	Cost/Unit	Cost
11/5	800	$10.00	$8,000
11/7	300	11.00	3,300
11/8	320	12.25	3,920
11/15	200	14.70	2,940
Total	1,620	N/A	$18,160

UNITS SOLD			
Date	# Units	Cost/Unit	Cost
11/10	750	Varies By	
11/14	460	Valuation	
11/18	220	Method	
Total	1,430	N/A	N/A

	Basic Events			FIFO Method of Accounting				
	Units Purchased			Units Sold			Ending Inventory	
Date	# Units	Cost/Unit	Total Cost	# Units	Cost/Unit	Total Cost	# Units	Total Cost
11/5	800	$ 10.00	$ 8,000				800	$ 8,000
11/7	300	11.00	3,300				1,100	11,300
11/8	320	12.25	3,920				1,420	15,220
11/10				750	$ 10.00	$ 7,500	670	7,720
11/14				50	10.00	500	620	7,220
				300	11.00	3,300	320	3,920
				110	12.25	1,348	210	2,573
11/15	200	14.70	2,940				410	5,513
11/18				210	12.25	2,573	200	2,940
				10	14.70	147	190	2,793

LIFO Method of Inventory Valuation:

	Basic Events			LIFO Method of Accounting				
	Units Purchased			Units Sold			Ending Inventory	
Date	# Units	Cost/Unit	Total Cost	# Units	Cost/Unit	Total Cost	# Units	Total Cost
11/5	800	$ 10.00	$ 8,000				800	$ 8,000
11/7	300	10.25	3,075				1,100	11,075
11/8	320	9.85	3,152				1,420	14,227
11/10				320	$ 9.85	$ 3,152	1,100	11,075
				300	10.25	3,075	800	8,000
				130	10.00	1,300	670	6,700
11/14				460	10.00	4,600	210	2,100
11/15	200	10.22	2,044				410	4,144
11/18				200	10.22	2,044	210	2,100
				20	10.00	200	190	1,900

Average Cost Method of Inventory Valuation:

Average Cost = Total Cost of Goods Available for Sale ÷ Total Quantity of Goods Available for Sale

= $18,160 ÷ 1,620 units

= $11.21/unit

Ending Inventory

	Basic Events			Average Cost Method of Accounting				
	Units Purchased			Units Sold			Ending Inventory	
Date	# Units	Cost/Unit	Total Cost	# Units	Cost/Unit	Total Cost	# Units	Total Cost
11/5	800	$ 10.00	$ 8,000				800	$ 8,000
11/7	300	11.00	3,300				1,100	11,300
11/8	320	12.25	3,920				1,420	15,220
11/10				750	$ 11.21	$ 8,407	670	813
11/14				460	11.21	5,157	210	1,656
11/15	200	14.70	2,940				410	4,596
11/18				220	11.21	2,466	190	2,130

Exhibit 2–2 Calculating Cost of Goods Sold

	FIFO	LIFO	Avg Cost Method
Cost of Goods Purchased	$18,160	$18,160	$18,160
Minus: Ending Inventory	2,793	1,900	2,130
Cost of Goods Sold	$15,367	$16,260	$16,030

resources, while liabilities and equity are how those resources are paid for.

- ▸ Assets represent a company's resources. Assets can be in the form of cash or other items that have monetary value, including inventory. Assets are made up of (a) current assets (cash assets or assets easily convertible to cash within one year, such as accounts receivable, securities, and inventory), (b) longer term assets such as investments and fixed assets (property/plant/equipment), or (c) intangible assets (patents, copyrights, and goodwill).

- ▸ Liabilities represent amounts owed to creditors (debt, accounts payable, and lease-term obligations).

- ▸ Equity represents ownership or rights to the assets of the company (common stock, additional paid-in capital, and retained earnings).

Inventory is typically counted among a company's *current assets* because it can be sold within one year. This information is used to calculate financial ratios that help assess the financial health of the company. Note, however, that the balance sheet is not the only place that inventory plays a role in the financial analysis of the company. In fact, inventory shows up on the income statement in the form of *cost of goods sold.*

Inventory on the Income Statement

The income statement is a report that identifies a company's revenues (sales), expenses, and resulting profits. While the balance sheet can be described as a snapshot of a company on a *specific date* (June 30, for example), the income statement covers *a given period of time* (June 1 through June 30). The *cost of goods* sold is the item on the income statement that reflects the cost of inventory flowing out of a business.

The old saying, "it costs money to make money," explains the cost of goods sold. You make money by using or selling inventory. That inventory costs you something. Cost of goods sold (on the income statement) represents the value of goods (inventory) sold during the accounting period. See Exhibit 2–3.

The value of goods that are not sold is represented by the ending inventory amount on the balance sheet calculated as:

Ending Inventory =
Beginning Inventory + Purchases – Cost of Goods Sold

This information is also useful because it can be used to show how a company "officially" accounts for inventory. With it, you can back into the cost of purchases without knowing the actual costs by turning around the equation as follows:

Purchases =
Ending Inventory – Beginning Inventory + Cost of Goods Sold

Or, you can figure out the cost of goods sold if you know what your purchases are by making the following calculation:

Cost of Goods Sold =
Beginning Inventory + Purchases – Ending Inventory

Finally, as you sell/use inventory and take in revenue for it, you subtract the cost of the items from the income. The result is your gross profit.

Ratio Analyses and What They Mean

Is something good or is it bad? To answer this question we often compare one thing to another. That is the definition of a "ratio"; it is an expression of how many of one item is contained within another.

Exhibit 2–3 Sample Balance Sheet and Income Statement

Balance Sheet (assumes FIFO Method of Accounting)

Assets		Liabilities and Equity	
Cash	$5,000	Accounts Payable	$10,000
Accounts Receivable	11,500	Notes Payable	7,500
Inventory		Current Portion of	
(per FIFO method)	2793	Long-Term Debt	3,050
Other Current Assets	7,000	Total Current Liabilities	20,550
Total Current Assets	26,293	Long-Term Debt	30,500
Investments	1,800	Long-Term	
Property, Plant, &		Lease Obligations	12,250
Equipment (net)	53,000	Total Liabilities	$63,300
Deferred Charges	1,000	Shareholders' Equity	$19,993
Patents, Goodwill	1,200	Total Liabilities	
Total Assets	$83,293	and Equity	$83,293

Income Statement	FIFO	LIFO	Avg. Cost Method
Revenues	$21,582	$21,582	$21,582
Less: Cost of Goods Sold	15,367	16,260	16,030
Gross Profit	6,215	5,322	5,552
Less: Selling, General, and Administrative Expenses	2,500	2,500	2,500
Depreciation and Amortization Expenses	1,250	1,250	1,250
Goodwill Expense	553	553	553
Profit Before Taxes	1,912	1,019	1,249
Less: Federal Income Tax (assume 40%)	765	408	500
After-Tax Income	$1,147	$611	$749

CONCLUSIONS

1. By valuing its inventory under the FIFO method of inventory valuation, this company would have earned an extra $536 or $398 in after-tax income than under the LIFO or Average Cost methods of inventory valuation, respectively.

2. By valuing its inventory under the LIFO method of inventory valuation, this company would pay $357 or $92 less in federal income taxes than under the FIFO or Average Cost methods of inventory valuation, respectively.

Ratios can be used in the business world by selecting parts of an organization's financial statements and comparing one set of financial conditions to another. A company's financial statements contain key aspects of the business. By reviewing these aspects, you can determine an organization's economic well-being. One way of reviewing these financial conditions is to compare one to another dividing one by the other. For example, if you had $200 in cash and $100 worth of debts, you could divide the cash (assets) by the debt (liabilities), which would result in a ratio of 2 to 1. In other words, you have twice as many assets as you do liabilities.

Ratios are useful tools to explain trends and summarize business results. Often third parties, such as banks, use ratios to determine a company's credit worthiness. By itself, a ratio holds little meaning. However, when compared to other industry and/or company-specific figures or standards, ratios can be powerful in helping to analyze your company's current and historical results. Companies in the same industry often have similar liquidity ratios or benchmarks, as they often have similar cost structures. Your company's ratios can be compared to:

1. Prior period(s)
2. Company goals or budget projections
3. Companies in your industry
4. Companies in other industries
5. Companies in different geographic regions

In particular, the following three ratios are useful when assessing inventory.

CURRENT RATIO

The current ratio assesses the organization's overall liquidity and indicates a company's ability to meet its short-term obligations. In other words, it measures whether or not a company will be able to pay its bills. Technically speaking, the current ratio indicates how many dollars of assets we have for each dollar of liabilities that we owe. The current ratio is calculated as follows:

Current Ratio = Current Assets ÷ Current Liabilities

Current Assets refers to assets that are in the form of cash or that are easily convertible to cash within one year, such as accounts receivable, securities, and inventory. *Current Liabilities* refers to liabilities that are due and payable within twelve months, such as accounts payable, notes payable, and short-term portion of long-term debt.

Standards for the current ratio vary from industry to industry. Companies in the service industry that carry little or no inventory typically have current ratios ranging from 1.1 to 1.3—that is, $1.10 to $1.30 in current assets for each dollar of current liabilities. Companies that carry inventory have higher current ratios. Manufacturing companies are included in this latter group and often have current ratios ranging from 1.6 to 2.0; not only do they have inventory in the form of finished goods ready for sale, but they also carry inventory of goods that are not yet ready for sale. Generally speaking, the longer it takes a company to manufacture the inventory and the more inventory it must keep on hand, the higher the current ratio.

What the Current Ratio Might Mean

A low current ratio may signal that a company has liquidity problems or has trouble meeting its short- and long-term obligations. In other words, the organization might be suffering from a lack of cash flow to cover operating and other expenses. As a result, accounts payable may be building at a faster rate than receivables. Note, however, that this is only an indicator and must be used in conjunction with other factors to determine the overall financial health of an organization. In fact, some companies can sustain lower-than-average current ratios because they move their inventory quickly and/or are quick to collect from their customers. Therefore, these companies have good cash flow.

A high current ratio is not necessarily desirable. It might indicate that the company is holding high-risk inventory or may be doing a bad job of managing its assets. For example, fashion retailers may have costly inventory, but they might also have significant trouble getting rid of the inventory, for example, if the wrong clothing line was selected. This makes it a high-risk company, forcing creditors to require a bigger financial cushion.

Further, if a high current ratio is a result of a very large cash account, it may be an indication that the company is not reinvesting its cash appropriately. Even if the current ratio looks fine, other factors must be taken into consideration, as liquidity problems might still exist. Since ratios look at quantity, not quality, it is important to look at what the current assets consist of to determine if they are made up of slow-moving inventory. To assess inventory's impact on liquidity, another test of liquidity should be taken into account, such as the Quick Ratio (or Acid Test).

QUICK RATIO OR ACID TEST

The quick ratio compares the organization's most liquid current assets to its current liabilities. The quick ratio is calculated as follows:

Quick Ratio = (Current Assets − Inventories) ÷ Current Liabilities

Assume that an industry that sells on credit has a quick ratio of at least 0.8. In other words, the company has at least 80¢ in liquid assets (likely in the form of accounts receivable) for every $1 of liabilities. Industries that have significant cash sales (such as grocery stores) tend to be even lower. As with the current ratio, a low quick ratio is an indicator of cash flow problems, while a high ratio may indicate poor asset management, as cash may be properly reinvested or accounts receivable levels are out of control. An organization's ability to promptly collect its accounts receivable has a significant impact on this ratio. The quicker the collection the more liquidity it has.

INVENTORY TURNOVER RATIO

The inventory turnover ratio measures, on average, how many times inventory is replaced over a period of time. In its simplest sense, an inventory turn occurs every time an item is received, is used or sold, and then is replaced. If an SKU came in twice during the year, was used/sold, and then replenished, that would be two turns per year. If this happened once per month, it would be twelve turns per year, and so forth.

Inventory turnover is an important measure since the ability to move inventory quickly directly impacts the company's liquidity. Inventory turnover is calculated as follows:

Inventory Turnover Ratio = Cost of Goods Sold ÷ Average Inventory

Essentially, when a product is sold, it is subtracted from inventory and transferred to cost of goods sold. Therefore, this ratio indicates how quickly inventory is moving for accounting purposes. It does not necessarily reflect how many times actual physical items were handled within the facility itself. This is true because the cost of goods sold number may include items you sold but never physically handled. For example, items that we purchase and then have drop shipped directly at our customer's site are never handled within our facility. A more accurate measure of how many times actual physical inventory turned within the site would be:

Actual Physical Inventory Turnover Ratio = Cost of Goods Sold from
Inventory Only ÷ Average Inventory

Note that if the inventory has increased or decreased significantly during the year, the average inventory for the year may be skewed and not accurately reflect your turnover ratio going forward. In addition, if the company uses the LIFO method of accounting, the ratio may be inflated because LIFO may undervalue the inventory.

Unlike the current ratio and quick ratio, the inventory turnover ratio does not adhere to a standard range. Organizations with highly perishable products can have inventory turns 30 times a year or more. Companies that retain large amounts of inventory or that require a long time to build their inventory might have turns only two or three times a year. In general, the overall trend in business today is to reduce carrying costs by limiting the amount of inventory in stock at any given time. As a result, both individual inventory turnovers and industry averages in this area have increased in recent years.

It is important to understand, however, that many factors can cause a low inventory turnover ratio. The company may be holding the wrong type of inventory, its quality may be lacking, or it may have sales/marketing issues.

Profit Margins

Another set of ratios a stockkeeper must understand, especially one in a for-profit environment, are those relating to profit margins.

Profit margins are ratios of profitability that measure how much out of every dollar of sales a company actually keeps in earnings. If a company's expenses increase more quickly than sales, then even though sales might be higher than sales during the same time period last year, its profit margins will go down. Basically, business owners use gross profit margins to:

▸ Set prices at levels that ensure a strong profit, or

▸ Measure and reduce costs for better profitability, or

▸ Determine what to charge for a new item to make it profitable.

CALCULATING GROSS PROFIT

Gross profit is the amount you have after you subtract all costs associated with a sale. To understand gross profit, it is important to know the distinction between *variable* and *fixed* costs. See Exhibit 2–4.

Exhibit 2–4 Variable and Fixed Costs

Variable costs are those that change based on the amount of product being made and are incurred as a direct result of producing the product. Variable costs include:	• Materials used • Direct labor • Packaging • Freight • Plant supervisors' salaries • Utilities for a plant or warehouse • Depreciation expense on production equipment and machinery
Fixed costs generally are more static in nature. They include:	• Office expenses, such as supplies, utilities, telephones, and computers • Salaries and wages of office staff, salespeople, and officers and owners • Payroll taxes and employee benefits • Advertising, promotional, and other sales expenses • Insurance • Auto expenses for salespeople • Professional fees • Rent
Variable expenses are recorded as cost of goods sold. *Fixed expenses* are counted as operating expenses (sometimes called selling and general and administrative expenses)	

To figure out your gross profit margin, you first need to calculate your gross profit. The formula for gross profit is:

Gross Profit = Sales − Cost of Goods Sold

Cost of goods sold (COGS) includes only the direct cost incurred to manufacture or sell a product.

COGS includes items:

▶ purchased for resale or

▶ used to manufacture a product (as well as the direct labor cost to produce the product).

COGS does not include operating expenses such as office rent, office utilities, and indirect labor.

By itself, gross profit doesn't mean much. However, by using it to calculate the *gross profit margin,* you can use it to spot profitability trends over time. The formula for gross profit margin is:

Gross Profit Margin = Gross Profit ÷ Sales x 100%

Example

Company X has gross sales for 2009 equaling $5 million. The cost of goods sold amounts to $1.2 million. What is the gross profit margin?

Gross Profit Margin = (5,000,000 − 1,200,000) ÷ 5,000,000
Gross Profit Margin = 3,800,000 ÷ 5,000,000
Gross Profit Margin = 76%

Company X has gross sales for 2010 equaling $5.5 million. The cost of goods sold amounts to $1.4 million. What is the gross profit margin?

Gross Profit Margin = (5,500,000 − 1,400,000) ÷ 5,500,000
Gross Profit Margin = 4,100,000 ÷ 5,500,000
Gross Profit Margin = 74%

So what: Companies that have a high gross profit margin have greater cash flow; and, those with stable or increasing gross profit margins are more profitable than those whose gross profit margins fluctuate wildly or decrease over time. In the example, although Company X had greater sales from one year to the next, its gross profit margin fell, indicating an increase in costs. If this trend continues, the company will be in trouble.

You should calculate gross profit margin when you review your monthly and quarterly financial statements because even if all costs are covered and net income is strong and growing, changes in gross profit margin can serve as early signs that an increase in COGS is eroding your profitability.

Gross profit margins for a given business can also be compared to the gross profit margins common in that industry to determine how the enterprise is doing. Don't compare one industry to another. Why? Because it is common in some industries to sell large quantities of goods at a low gross profit margin, while in others smaller quantities at larger gross profit margins are more normal.

You can use a combination of approaches to increase your business's gross profit margins, including:

▸ Increase the number of units sold (sales volume).

▸ Reduce elements of COGS, for example, by substituting less expensive materials and automating to use less labor.

▸ Raise prices. Try different pricing strategies until your gross profit margin reaches the desired level. See Exhibit 2–5.

Exhibit 2–5 Pricing Strategies

Skimming	• A short-term profit strategy. Skimming means charging a relatively high price for a short time when a new, innovative, or much-improved product is brought to market. • The idea is to "skim off" customers who are willing to pay a premium price to obtain the item right away. • This strategy works well for "conspicuous" or "prestige items," such as a new type of electronic device. • Prices are lowered later when demand from the early buyers falls.
Market Penetration Pricing	• Short-term profit strategy—selling at the lowest possible price for a short-term period. • Often used to introduce a new product or business with an expected long-term life cycle.
Loss Leader Pricing	• Purposely pricing some products at a level that eliminates profit. • Done to increase customer traffic.
Price Lining	• Grouping products at certain price points (e.g., all items for $9.99). • Makes shopping easy for the consumer and averages out desired markup.
Price Bundling	• Selling a product in multiple units (e.g., "Two for the price of one" or "Buy three and receive one free").
Status Quo Pricing	• Price levels are firmly established and remain relatively fixed until something happens in the marketplace that requires a change or adjustment.

Merchandising Metrics

Stockkeepers, especially those in for-profit enterprises, often must be concerned with setting the right price for an item or a grouping of items. Or, they must determine the cost of an item.

PRICING GENERALLY

Price setting begins with determining the *breakeven point.*

▸ The *breakeven point* is reached when the cost of producing/purchasing and/or selling a product or service is covered.

▸ The *contributing margin* is the gross profit derived from the sale of the product, that is, the selling price less the cost of the goods or materials.

Selling Price – Cost of Goods = Contributing Margin
$10 $6 $4

Breakeven Formula

At the breakeven point, the revenue and the total cost are equal.

Fixed Costs ÷ Contributing Margin = Breakeven Point
$100,000 ÷ $4   = 25,000 Units

SELLING PRICE

Price determination, the selling price, for many consumer products is often a function of the cost of production and a desired level of markup.

Margins, Markups, and Markdowns

A *profit margin* is different than a *markup.* The *margin* is the percentage of the final selling price that is profit. A *markup* is what percentage of the cost price you add to the cost price to get the selling price. A *markdown* is the difference between the original selling price and the price at which an item is actually sold.

A selling price with a margin of 25% results in more profit than a selling price with a markup of 25%. For example, if you buy an item for $100 and mark it up 25%, it would sell for $125. However, if you want to make a 25% (profit) margin it would sell for $133.33.

Determining the Selling Price

To calculate the *selling price at a percent margin when the cost is known,* divide the cost by 100 percent minus the desired margin percent.

Cost ÷ (100% – Markup Percent) = Selling Price

Examples:

Cost + (100% – Markup Percent)	= Selling Price
$5 + (100% – 50%) =	$10
$5 + (100% – 40%) =	$8.33
$5 + (100% – 20%) =	$6.25

A quicker way to work it out is to divide the cost by the profit margin you want to make. For example:

For a 5% margin, divide the cost price by 0.95
For a 10% margin, divide the cost price by 0.9
For a 15% margin, divide the cost price by 0.85
For a 20% margin, divide the cost price by 0.8
For a 25% margin, divide the cost price by 0.75
For a 30% margin, divide the cost price by 0.7

Examples:

For a 50% profit: $5 + .5 = $10
For a 40% profit: $5 + .6 = $8.33
For a 20% profit: $5 + .8 = $6.25

Determining the Cost

To calculate the *cost when the selling price and the markup percent are known,* multiply the selling price by the markup percent and subtract the answer from the selling price.

(Selling Price × Markup Percent) – Selling Price = Cost

Example

($10 Selling Price x 40% Markup Percent) = $4 Markup
$10 Selling Price – $4 Markup   = $6 Cost

Determining the Margin Percent

To determine the *margin percent when the cost and the selling price are known,* subtract the cost from the selling price. Divide the difference by the selling price.

(Selling Price – Cost) + Selling Price = Margin Percent

Example

$10 Selling Price – $6 Cost = $4 Profit
$4 + $10 = 0.4 or 40% Margin

Determining Markdowns (on Sale Price)

Sometimes an item does not sell at the desired price. You must then sell it at a *markdown.* In other words, you're going to put the item "on sale."

To determine the *marked-down (on-sale) price where the original price and the markdown percent are known,* multiply the original price by the markdown percent. Subtract the answer from the original price.

Original Price – (Original Price x Percent Markdown) =
On-Sale Price

Example

$10 Original Price x 15% Markdown) = $1.50 Markdown
$10 Original Price − $1.50 Markdown = $8.50 Sale Price

Determining Net Operating Profit Before Taxes

A measure of a company's profitability is its *net operating profit.*
Net operating profit is the profitability of a company after accounting for cost of goods sold and operating expenses. Operating profit
does not include expenses such as interest and taxes. See Exhibit
2–6. It also doesn't depend on capital structure or one-time expenses. So, it really does measure how well an enterprise is doing.

Exhibit 2–6 Calculating Net Operating Profit Before Taxes

The profit and expense for each dollar sold is calculated as
follows:

Sales price	$1.00
Cost of Product	− 0.50
Freight Cost	− 0.02
Gross Profit	0.48
Operating Expenses	− 0.34
Net Operating Profit Before Taxes	0.14

Obsolete Stock

Any stockkeeper who has had to repeatedly move really slow moving or outright dead stock out of the way or finds herself hurting
for space because obsolete product eats up square foot after square
foot knows that these items "just gotta go."

WHY YOU HAVE BEEN TOLD NOT TO DISPOSE OF OBSOLETE STOCK

Why is the dead stock still here? The three reasons most often given as to why the product can't be disposed of are:

1. It's already paid for.
2. We might use it someday.
3. We might sell it someday.

These explanations seem logical, and the idea of throwing away dead stock may be counterintuitive. However, there are some very real practical problems with simply hauling it off to the dumpster.

PROBLEMS WITH CONVINCING DECISION MAKERS THAT "ITS GOTTA GO"

Decision makers often have difficulty with disposing of dead inventory because it will adversely impact the balance sheet and deplete resources considered to be valuable for lending purposes.

Impact of Write-Off

Anything that appears as an asset on the balance sheet has an accounting value. This value, consisting of an item's original cost minus depreciation, is called the "book value." It is irrelevant that the item may actually be worthless to either a customer or as part of a manufacturing process. If it has a one-dollar value on the books, then disposing of dead inventory has an accounting consequence to our organization.

If we sell dead inventory that has a monetary value at a deep discount, throw it away, or give it away to a charity, we will have to immediately write off the book value of those items, which will, of course, have a negative impact on the financial statements.

If your organization is sensitive to making extraordinary adjustments to the balance sheet and never or seldom writes off dead inventory, you may have a difficult time ever convincing any decision maker to dispose of these items. The decision maker will simply not be willing to "take the hit on the books."

Organization's Capital Structure

Almost everyone has heard the expression, "cash is king." The problem for many organizations is that cash flow doesn't always keep up with needs.

Often organizations raise operating capital by borrowing against (a) their accounts receivable and (b) the book value of the inventory they are carrying.

"Accounts receivable" are the amounts due from customers resulting from normal sales activities. Depending on the industry, banks will generally lend up to 75 percent of the value of accounts receivable due in 90 days or less.

Bankers will also lend against the book value of inventory. The willingness to lend against this asset is not as straightforward as with accounts receivable. The more complex nature of these transactions comes from the fact that in accordance with accepted accounting practices, we should value inventory at the lower of cost or fair market value. Therefore, dead stock should logically be valued at a fair market value of zero dollars no matter what it originally cost.

In spite of generally accepted accounting practices and even though parts of your inventory have no real market value (and should be valued at zero dollars), bankers will often loan your organization 50 to 60 percent of the value of the inventory as that value is shown on the books. So, companies will sometimes continue to carry dead stock so as to retain this artificial value on the books. This is an area most stockkeepers will not have any direct control over. However, the arguments below may overcome the need to keep inventory values artificially high.

ARGUMENTS IN FAVOR OF DISPOSING OF DEAD STOCK

Strong arguments can be made in favor of disposing of nonproductive stock, including recapture of space, better use of labor and equipment, and a reduction in the costs associated with having inventory sitting around.

Recapture of Space

In terms of space utilization, there are some simple mathematical facts to keep in mind:

▸ Multiplying an item's length by its width tells you the amount of square feet the item is occupying.

▸ Multiplying an item's length by its width by its height tells you the amount of cubic space it is occupying.

If you were to actually figure out the cubic space taken up by dead product, you would gain a powerful argument in favor of disposing of this inventory. To bolster the argument, you may want to ask your organization's financial officer how much the company is paying per square foot for rent. Multiplying the square footage being consumed by dead product by the rent per square foot often results in a truly eye-opening dollar amount. Providing actual numbers to a decision maker is far more effective than speaking in generalities, such as "dead stock is taking up a lot of space." Pointing out that obsolete stock is "taking up 4,000 square feet" or "represents $2,000 per month in per square foot costs" should help you convince your decision maker that "its gotta go."

Efficient Utilization of Labor and Machine Resources

Not only does obsolete inventory take up a lot of space, it can also get in the way of workers. Repeatedly moving obsolete product out of the way hurts efficient use of both labor and machine time.

Too often, in trying to argue against keeping obsolete stock, stockkeepers will state generalities, such as "it takes us a lot of time to move that stuff around." How long is "a lot of time"? Is it an hour a day, four hours per week? Without specific numbers, your arguments will sound hollow.

As many business writers have noted, "You cannot control what you do not measure." There are two things you need to do to get specific time and dollar amounts:

▶ During each week for one month, every time you or your staff move dead product out of the way, measure the amount of direct labor that goes into that effort. Remember, if two workers are working together to move the items and they work for fifteen minutes, that represents fifteen minutes times two, or thirty minutes of direct labor.

▶ At the end of the month, divide the total amount of labor hours by four to determine a weekly average. To determine the amount of yearly labor involved in moving dead stock, multiply the weekly average times the number of weeks in a year your company operates.

Once again, obtain base information from your financial officer and multiply the average hourly wage you pay your workers, including benefits, by the annual labor number. The result will make a rather impressive argument as to how the organization can save thousands of dollars per year by disposing of its dead stock.

Reduction of Carrying Costs (K Factor)

The K Factor represents the number of pennies per inventory dollar per year a company is spending to house its inventory. It is generally expressed as a percentage. In other words, a K Factor of 25 percent means that you are spending 25¢ per inventory dollar per year to house your inventory. A $1 dead item that sits on your shelf for a year would cost you 25¢ that year, a total of 50¢ at the end of the second year, a total of 75¢ at the end of the third year, and so on.

There are two ways of computing the K Factor—a traditional method in which you add together various expenses directly related to carrying inventory and a rough rule-of-thumb method. See Exhibit 2–7.

Since it always costs something to carry inventory, it is obvious that the longer dead stock remains in your facility, the more it will cost. Two approaches can be used to effectively argue this point:

1. Demonstrate the impact of carrying costs on your existing dead stock. This addresses the "We've already paid for it," argument in favor of retaining dead stock. See Exhibit 2–8 and Exhibit 2–9.

2. Demonstrate that if the product remains long enough, even selling it at a profit will not Recapture your original cost. This addresses the "We might need it someday" and "We might sell it someday" arguments in favor of retaining dead stock. See Exhibit 2–10.

In Exhibit 2–8 a percentage is used to indicate the amount of dead stock in the facility. Note, however, it is always more convincing to a decision maker if you use actual lists and dollar amounts to demonstrate those items that are dead rather than using a generality like a rough percentage. See Exhibit 2–9.

Exhibit 2–7 Methods of Determining the Cost of Carrying Inventory

Traditional Accounting Method		Rule-of-Thumb Method
Warehouse Space	$130,000	20% + Prime Lending Rate
Taxes	65,000	= K Factor
Insurance	40,000	
Obsolescence/Shrinkage	23,000	
Material Handling	64,800	
Cost of Money Invested	200,000	
Total Annual Costs	$522,800	

$$\frac{\text{Total Annual Costs}}{\text{Avg Inventory Value}} = \frac{\$522,800}{\$2,000,000} = 26\% \text{ K Factor}$$

Exhibit 2–8 Demonstrating the Impact of the K Factor on Existing Dead Stock

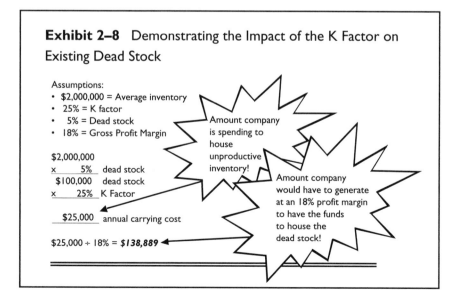

Assumptions:
- $2,000,000 = Average inventory
- 25% = K factor
- 5% = Dead stock
- 18% = Gross Profit Margin

```
  $2,000,000
x        5%   dead stock
   $100,000   dead stock
x       25%   K Factor

    $25,000   annual carrying cost

$25,000 ÷ 18% = $138,889
```

Amount company is spending to house unproductive inventory!

Amount company would have to generate at an 18% profit margin to have the funds to house the dead stock!

Exhibit 2–9 Creating an Inventory Analysis Report Listing Dead Stock

SKU #	DESCRIPTION	QUANT ON HAND	UNIT COST	DOLLAR VALUE OF PRODUCT IN-HOUSE	MONTHLY USAGE	PROJECTED ANNUAL USAGE	MONTHS SUPPLY ON HAND

METHODS OF DISPOSAL

Various approaches to disposing of dead stock exist:

▶ Sell at net price

▶ Temporarily raise commissions for salespeople

▶ Discount the price

▶ Return to vendor

▶ Donate it

▶ Write it off

▶ Auction

It is important to remember something about convincing decision makers of anything. Ordinarily, when reports or other information flow up a chain of command, the level of detail at each level decreases. Generally, each higher level of management wants to see less and less information with which to make decisions. You should resist providing only minimal data in making arguments regarding dead stock. This is a time to let the details do the talking.

Exhibit 2–10 Demonstrating the Impact of the K Factor on Items Sold at a Profit but after Remaining in Stock for Long Periods of Time

Assumptions:
- 720 pairs of earmuffs purchased at $2.25 per pair ($1,620 original cost)
- Earmuffs have remained unsold for 2 years
- We hope to sell at a 30% gross profit per pair ($2.93 pair)
- 25% K factor

$1,620 x 25% = $405 per year in carrying cost

$405 ÷ 720 pairs = 56¢ per year, per pair
in additional carrying cost expense

Additional cost after one year:
$2.25 + $0.56 = $2.81/pair (720 pairs x $2.81/pair = $2,023)

Additional cost after two years:
$2.81 + $0.56 = $3.37/pair (720 pairs x $3.37/pair = $2,426)

Costs are going up $0.002 per day ($0.56 ÷ 365 days/yr)

$2.93   sales price
−2.25   original cost
$0.68   gross profit expected

$0.68 ÷ $0.002 = breakeven at 340 days—after 340 days there is no profit at all!

Original cost: $2,500

Cost including carrying costs after two years:
$4,449 ($2,023 + $2,426)
Revenue from selling earmuffs at $2.93/pair: $2,110
($2.93/pair x 720 pairs)

Loss on sale made after inventory has been in-house for two years even though sale made at 30% gross profit on original cost: $2,339

Carrying Cost and Purchasing

Although you should only have the minimum amount of inventory on hand required for either production or distribution, be careful not to purchase small quantities over and over again. Buying small amounts frequently will lead to an excessive cost of replenishment (the "R Factor").

A simple example of how an excessive R Factor can be created would be the following:

Example

Assumptions:

It costs a certain amount of money per line item, per purchase order to buy something. Assume $2.59 per line item, per purchase order for this example.

You Purchase 1 million widgets per year.

If you bought all 1 million widgets at one time, the R Factor would be $2.59, since there was only one purchase order with one line item on it.

If you bought 250,000 widgets at a time, the R Factor would be $10.36. That is because you would have four purchase orders with one line item each at a cost of $2.59 each.

If you bought 1 million widgets one at a time at an R Factor of $2.59 each the replenishment cost would be $2,590,000!

Because of the R Factor, modern purchasing dictates that you buy larger quantities on fewer purchase orders, but with suppliers releasing items on a prearranged schedule or on demand.

Ultimately, the point at which your cost of carrying inventory matches the cost of purchasing it is the proper economic order quantity of that item. See "Replenishment Costs" in Chapter 5, Planning and Replenishment Concepts.

Recap

The objective of this chapter was to provide you with highlights of the most basic accounting concepts you, as a stockkeeper, must understand to successfully discuss and plan inventory values with your colleagues.

Although you may never participate in the preparation of month- or year-end financial statements, it is in your own self-interest to review these statements and think about how the inventory values reflected impact your operation.

Also, regular, detailed examination of your gross profit margin and how its components change over time can assist you in highlighting opportunities for improvement in operations and profitability.

And finally, whenever discussing either buying more stock or getting rid of dead stock, it is always more persuasive to use actual numbers than to deal in generalities. Remember, "if you can measure it, you can control it."

REVIEW QUESTIONS

1. A balance sheet is best described as:
   (a) A report that identifies a company's revenues (sales), expenses, and resulting profits for a given period of time.
   (b) A report that shows the financial position of a company on a specific date.
   (c) A report that shows the relationship between inventory on hand and on order.
   (d) A report that identifies the number of items per level and number of tiers of product on a pallet.

2. An income statement is best described as:
   (a) A report that identifies a company's revenues (sales), expenses, and resulting profits for a given period of time.
   (b) A report that shows the financial position of a company on a specific date.
   (c) A report that shows the relationship between inventory on hand and on order.
   (d) A report that identifies the number of items per level and number of tiers of product on a pallet.

3. True or False

   The K Factor represents the number of pennies per inventory dollar per year a company is spending to house its inventory.
   (a) True
   (b) False

4. True or False

   The K Factor is generally expressed as a percentage.
   (a) True
   (b) False

5. Current Assets ÷ Current Liabilities is the formula for which ratio?
   (a) Inventory Turn Ratio
   (b) Current Ratio
   (c) Quick Ratio

Answers
1. (b), 2. (a), 3. (a), 4. (a), 5. (b)

CHAPTER 3

PHYSICAL LOCATION AND CONTROL OF INVENTORY

I f you can't find an item, you can't count it, fill an order with it, or build a widget with it. If you cannot control the location of your product or raw materials from both physical and recordkeeping standpoints, then your inventory accuracy will suffer.

To sustain inventory accuracy on an ongoing basis you must:

▸ Formalize the overall locator system used throughout the facility

▸ Track the storage and movement of product from

 • Receipt to storage

 • Order filling to shipping, or to staging at a point-of-use

▸ Maintain timely records of all item storage and movement

The objective of this chapter is to give you guidance in setting up a system that allows you to put items where they will do the most good for your organization. It will provide you with a working knowledge of (1) three key stock locator systems (which relate to the overall organization of SKUs within a facility and their impact on space planning); (2) item placement theories dealing with the specific arrangement of products within an area of the warehouse (should the box be over here or over there?); and (3) some practical methods of attaching addresses to stock items and how to tie an item number to its location address.

Common Locator Systems

The purpose of a material locator system is to create procedures that allow you to track product movement throughout the facility. Although going by many names, the most common "pure" systems are *memory, fixed,* and *random.* A type of fixed system is the zone system. The *combination* approach is a common mixture of the fixed and random systems.

In considering which locator system will work best, you should attempt to maximize:

- ▶ Use of space
- ▶ Use of equipment
- ▶ Use of labor
- ▶ Accessibility to all items
- ▶ Protection from damage
- ▶ Ability to locate an item
- ▶ Flexibility
- ▶ The reduction of administrative costs

Maximizing all of these considerations at the same time is difficult, if not impossible. Often, each of these concerns creates conflicts with one or more of the others. For example, you may wish to store all cylinders together to utilize the same equipment to handle them or locate them together for ease of reach and retrieval. However, if the chemical nature of the contents of these cylinders prohibits them from being stored in the same area, safety and pro-

tection of property concerns take precedence over other consideration-
ations. Exhibit 3–1 provides scenarios in which several valid considerations are in conflict.

The stockkeeper should select a locator system that provides
the best solution given the tradeoffs between conflicting objectives.
No one system is "right." What is best will depend on considerations such as:

▸ Space available

▸ Location system (See the "Impact on Physical Space"
  sections in this chapter.)

▸ Dimensions of product or raw materials stored

▸ Shape of items

▸ Weight of items

▸ Product characteristics, such as stackable, toxic, liquid,
  crushable

▸ Storage methods, such as floor stacked, racks, carousels,
  shelving

▸ Labor availability

▸ Equipment, including special attachments available

▸ Information systems support

Every company has a limited amount of space available for
stock storage. Some locator systems use space more effectively than
do others. When choosing your locator system, think carefully
about how much space it will use. The following pages discuss several types of locator systems and evaluate the strengths and weaknesses of each.

MEMORY SYSTEMS

The most fundamental of all locator systems is the "memory" system.

Exhibit 3–1 Examples of Valid Storage Considerations in Conflict

• Scenario One—*Accessibility versus Space:* Charmax, Inc. wishes to have its entire product as easy to get to as possible for order filling purposes. It therefore attempted to have a "picking face" (a front-line, visible position from which the product can easily be selected) for each item. In order to actually create a picking face for each SKU, Charmax would have to assign a specific location for every product appearing on all of its pick tickets, with no two items being placed one on top of another, and no item being placed behind another. Charmax quickly realized that it lacked sufficient space in its facility to have a specific position for every item it carried.

• Scenario Two—*Use of Labor versus Protection from Damage:* Alana Banana Enterprises wishes to reduce labor hours by putting into place efficient product handling procedures. Its intent is to develop standard operating procedures so that workers will only handle SKUs four times: once when it is received, once when stored, once when picked, and once when loaded. However, in order to protect SKUs from bruising, items must be placed into protective cartons for storage. SKUs are not picked in full carton quantities so workers have to remove various quantities at different times from the cartons. Empty cartons must then be stacked, cleaned, restacked, and taken back to the receiving area for reuse. These protective measures add a number of labor-intensive steps to the process.

• Scenario Three—*Ability to Locate an Item versus Space Utilization:* Racquetballers America wants to assign a specific home to each of its products for inventory control purposes.

However, it has a small stockroom. Racquetballers realizes that if it uses a fixed storage location approach it must assign sufficient space to store the maximum amount of any one of its SKUs that will ever be on hand at one time in that location. If it uses a random location approach where items can be placed one on top of another or behind one another, then it will maximize its use of space. Racquetballers decides using its limited space is more important than putting in the extra labor and administration necessary to keep track of where everything is as it moves around the floor.

Basic Concept

Memory systems are solely dependent on human recall. Often, they are little more than someone saying, "I think it's over there."

The foundations of this locator system are simplicity, relative freedom from paperwork or data entry, and maximum utilization of all available space. Memory systems depend directly on people and only work if several or all of the conditions listed in Exhibit 3–2 exist at the same time.

Impact on Physical Space

The most complete space utilization is available through this system. Why? Because no item has a dedicated location that would prevent other SKUs from occupying that same stock location position if it were empty (either side-to-side or up-and-down).

Pros

As with all locator systems, the memory system has a number of strengths and weaknesses. Some of the pros are:

Exhibit 3–2 Conditions Under Which Memory Systems Will Work

- Storage locations are limited in number.
- Storage locations are limited in size.
- The variety of items stored in a location is limited.
- The size, shape, or unitization (e.g., palletization, strapping together, banding, etc.) of items allows for easy visual identification and separation of one SKU from another.
- Only one or a very limited number of individuals work within the storage areas.
- Workers within the storage area do not have duties that require them to be away from those locations.
- The basic types of items making up the inventory does not radically change within short time periods.
- There is not a lot of stock movement.

- ▶ Simple to understand
- ▶ Little or no ongoing paper-based or computer-based tracking required
- ▶ Full utilization of space
- ▶ No requirement for tying a particular stocking location, identifier, bin, slot, drawer, rack, bay, or spot to a specific SKU
- ▶ Requirements of single item facilities (such as a grain silo) can be met

Cons

Some negative aspects of a memory system are:

- The organization's ability to function must strongly rely on the memory, health, availability, and attitude of a single individual (or a small group of people)
- Significant and immediate decreases in accuracy result from changes in the conditions set out in Exhibit 3–2
- Once an item is lost to recall, it is lost to the system

Despite its limitations, a memory system may be as efficient as any other, particularly if there are only a limited number of different SKUs within a small area.

FIXED LOCATION SYSTEMS

Memory systems, in which nothing has a home and everything can be put wherever there's room, are at one extreme of locator systems. Fixed locator systems are at the other extreme.

Basic Concept

In pure fixed location systems, every item has a home and nothing else can live there. Some (not pure) fixed systems allow two or more items to be assigned to the same location, with only those items being stored there.

Impact on Physical Space

If quantities of any given SKU are large, then its "home" may consist of two or more storage positions. However, collectively all of these positions are the only places where this item may exist within the facility, and no other items may reside there. Basically, everything has a home and nothing else can live there.

Fixed location systems require large amounts of space for two reasons :

- Honeycombing

▶ Planning around the largest quantity of an item that will be in the facility at one time

Honeycombing is the warehousing situation where available storage space is not being fully utilized. Honeycombing is unavoidable given location system tradeoffs, product shape, and so on. The goal of a careful layout is to minimize how often and to what extent this happens.

Honeycombing occurs both horizontally (side-to-side) and vertically (up-and-down), robbing us of both square feet and cubic space. See Exhibit 3–3.

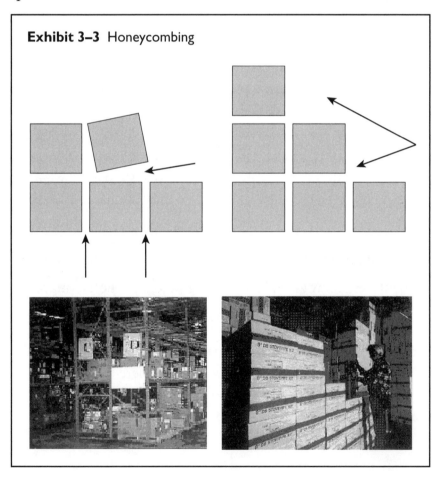

Exhibit 3–3 Honeycombing

Cause	Description
• Product shape	Physical characteristics cut down on stackability and prevent use of cubic space or placing one item against another.
• Product put away	Product not stacked or placed in a uniform manner, causing loss of vertical and horizontal space.
• Location system rules	A location is empty because no other item may be placed there as it is not the second item's assigned home.
• Poor housekeeping	Trash, poorly placed desks, etc., force empty space around it.

Two simple methods can determine the level of honeycombing within your own facility. One deals with a simple ratio analysis, the other with cubic space. See Exhibits 3–4 and 3–5.

The second reason the fixed system requires significant space is the necessity of planning around the largest quantity of an item that will be in the facility at one time. Each SKU will have an assigned location or locations. This "home" must be large enough to contain the total cubic space the item will fill up at the time that the largest quantity of that item will be in the facility. In other words, if a thousand cases of widgets are in the warehouse at the same time, the home of the widgets has to be large enough to hold them all. Therefore, the total space required for all items in a fixed system will be the total cubic space of one hundred percent of all SKUs, as though the maximum quantity of each of them was in the facility at one time. Space planning for an entire inventory in a dedicated location environment is planned around a one-year time period. Stated differently, all of the space needed for all of the widgets has to be added to all of the space needed for the gidgits and that space has to be added to all of the room needed for the doodads, and so on.

Exhibit 3–4 Determining Impact of Honeycombing—Ratio Method

Determine the impact of honeycombing on your present facility.

1. Count the number of locations you currently have set up to store items—both horizontally and vertically. Include all locations whether full, partially full, or empty.

2. Count the number of empty positions.

3. Divide the number of empty locations by the total storage positions you have. The result will be your honeycombing ratio.

$$\frac{\text{Honeycombing}}{\text{Ratio}} = \frac{\text{Empty Storage Locations}}{\text{Total Storage Locations}}$$

Example: $\dfrac{847}{1,200}$ = .294 or about 30% Honeycombing Ratio

That ratio represents the percentage of empty space within the storage portion of your stockroom(s). Determining this ratio provides you with a baseline. If you decide to change your storage philosophy, change your storage mechanisms (for example, from racks to floor stacking, or from racks to shelving). You can then determine the new ratio and measure improvement in space utilization.

Exhibit 3–5 Determining Impact of Honeycombing—Square Footage Method

Globus, Inc. has 16,000 cubic feet (ft³) of storage space. Globus has a fixed locator system and has divided the storeroom into 490 storage locations with the following sizes (and empty locations):

No. of Locations	Ft³	Total Cu Ft	Empty Locations
400	20	8,000	65
50	50	2,500	15
25	100	2,500	5
15	200	3,000	8
490		16,000	93

The honeycombing ratio on a location basis is:

$$\frac{\text{Empty Spaces}}{\text{Total Spaces}} = \frac{93}{490} = 19\%$$

The honeycombing ratio on a ft³ basis is:

$$\frac{\text{Empty Spaces} \times \text{ft}^3}{\text{Total ft}^3} = \frac{(65 \times 20 \text{ ft}^3) + (50 \times 15 \text{ ft}^3) + (5 \times 100 \text{ ft}^3) + (8 \times 200 \text{ ft}^3)}{16{,}000 \text{ ft}^3}$$

$$= \frac{1{,}300 + 750 + 500 + 1{,}600}{16{,}000}$$

$$= \frac{4{,}150}{16{,}000}$$

$$= 26\%$$

(continues)

(Exhibit 3-5 Continued.)

> The ratio method is a relatively simple approach to determining a rough estimate of honeycombing. However, the ratio method doesn't account for the fact that storage spaces within a given facility come in various sizes. A more precise method to determine honeycombing is to calculate the amount of unused cubic feet.

Pros

Fixed locator systems have the following definite advantages:

▸ Immediate knowledge of where all items are located. (This system feature dramatically reduces confusion as to "where to put it" and "where to find it," which increases efficiency and productivity, while reducing errors in both stocking and order fulfillment.)

▸ Training time for new hires and temporary workers is reduced.

▸ Simplifies and expedites both receiving and stock replenishment because predetermined put-away instructions can be generated.

▸ Allows for controlled routing of order fillers.

▸ Allows product to be aligned sequentially (for example, SKU001, SKU002, SKU003).

▸ Allows for strong control of individual lots, facilitating *first in first out* ("FIFO") control, if that is desired. Lot control can also be accomplished under a random location system. However simpler, more definitive control is possible using the dedicated location concept.

▸ Allows product to be positioned close to its ultimate point-of-use. Product positioning is discussed in the "Item Placement Theories" section of this chapter.

▸ Allows product to be placed in a location most suitable to an SKU's size, weight, toxic nature, flammability, or other similar characteristics.

Cons

Are there disadvantages to fixed locator systems? Of course. Chief among the cons are:

▸ Contributes to honeycombing within storage areas.

▸ Space planning must allow for the total cubic volume of all products likely to be in a facility within a defined period of time.

▸ Dedicated systems are somewhat inflexible. If you have aligned product by sequential numbering and then add a subpart or delete a numbered SKU, then you must move all products to allow for the add-in or collapse out locations to fill in the gap.

▸ Basically, fixed or dedicated location systems allow for strong control over items without the need to constantly update location records. That control must be counterbalanced by the amount of physical space required by this system.

ZONING SYSTEMS

A variation of pure fixed locator systems are those that place similar items in "zones."

Basic Concept

Zoning is centered around an item's characteristics. Like a fixed system, only items with certain characteristics can live in a particular area. Items with different attributes can't live there.

An SKU's characteristics would cause the item to be placed within a certain area of the stockroom or at a particular level within a section of shelving or rack section. See Exhibit 3–6. For example, irregular-shaped SKUs might be placed in lower levels to ease handling, or all items requiring the use of a forklift for put away or retrieval might be located in a specific area and on pallets.

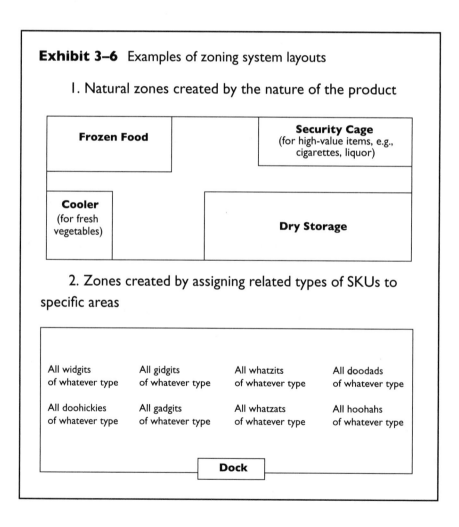

Exhibit 3–6 Examples of zoning system layouts

1. Natural zones created by the nature of the product

Frozen Food		Security Cage (for high-value items, e.g., cigarettes, liquor)
Cooler (for fresh vegetables)		Dry Storage

2. Zones created by assigning related types of SKUs to specific areas

All widgits of whatever type	All gidgits of whatever type	All whatzits of whatever type	All doodads of whatever type
All doohickies of whatever type	All gadgits of whatever type	All whatzats of whatever type	All hoohahs of whatever type

Dock

Impact on Physical Space

As with dedicated systems the more tightly you control where a particular item will be stored, the more you will contribute to honeycombing or to the need to plan around maximum quantities.

Pros

Some of the pros of using zoning systems are:

▶ Allows for the isolation of SKUs according to such characteristics as size, variety, flammability, toxicity, weight, lot control, private labeling, and so on.

▶ Allows for flexibility moving items from one zone to another quickly or in creating different zones efficiently.

▶ Allows for the addition of SKUs within a zone (unlike a fixed system) without having to move significant amounts of product to create room within an assigned location or within a sequentially numbered group of items. It also does not require the collapsing of space if an item is deleted.

▶ Allows for flexibility in planning: Although items are assigned to a general zone, because they do not have a specific position they must reside in, there is no need to plan around one hundred percent of any given item's cubic requirements.

Cons

As with any locator system, zoning systems also have a number of negative features, including:

▶ Zoning is not always required for efficient product handling. You may be adding needless administrative complexity by utilizing zoning.

▸ Zoning may contribute to honeycombing.

▸ Zoning requires updating of stock movement information.

Basically, zoning allows for control of item placement based on whatever characteristics the stockkeeper feels are important.

RANDOM LOCATOR SYSTEMS

Random locator systems allow for good space utilization but require more administration.

Basic Concept

In a random system nothing has a home, but you know where everything is. Pure random locator systems allow for the maximization of space since no item has a fixed home and may be placed wherever there is space. This allows SKUs to be placed above or in front of one another and for multiple items to occupy a single bin/slot/position/rack. The primary characteristic of a random locator system that makes it different from a memory system is that each SKU identifier is tied to whatever location address it is in while it is there. In other words, memory systems tie nothing together, except in the mind of the stockkeeper. Random systems have the flexibility of a memory system coupled with the control of a fixed or zone system. Essentially an item can be placed anywhere so long as its location is accurately noted in a computer database or a manually maintained paper-based card file system. When the item moves, it is deleted from that location. Therefore, an SKU's address is the location it is in while it is there.

Impact on Physical Space

Because items may be placed wherever there is space for them, random locator systems provide us with the best use of space and maximum flexibility while still allowing control over where an item can be found.

Planning space around a random locator system is generally based on the cubic space required for the average number of SKUs on hand at any one time. Therefore, in planning space requirements around a random locator system, you need to discern from our inventory records what our average inventory levels are and what products are generally present within that average. By multiplying the cubic footage of each of those items by the quantity of each usually on hand, you can determine our space required. See Exhibit 3–7.

Pros

The major reasons to consider using a random locator system are:
Maximization of space.
Control of where all items are at any given time.

Cons

Major concerns regarding the use of random locator systems are:
Constant updating of information is necessary to track where each item is at any given time. Updating must be accomplished through manual paper-based recording, bar code scanning, or intensive data entry updating.

May be unnecessarily complicated if your organization has a small number of SKUs.

Basically, random locator systems force a tradeoff between maximization of space and minimization of administration.

Exhibit 3-7 Planning a Storage Area Around a Fixed or a Random Locator System

Hammer Company manufactures widgits. It has broken down its bill-of-materials, the listing of all of the pieces and parts required to build a widgit, and has come up with the following list:

SKU #	Description	Container	Dimensions	Total Cubic Ft	Maximum Expected At One Time	Total Cubic Ft Req Fixed System	Total Ft Space Req Random System
12345	Gidgit	Box	2'x3'x1'	6 cu ft	50	300	90
54321	Whazzit	Carton	4'x4'x4'	64 cu ft	100	6,400	1,920
67890	Whozzit	Case	3'x4'x2'	24 cu ft	25	600	180
09876	Doodad	Box	2'x3'x1'	6 cu ft	50	300	90
					7,600	2,280	

If Hammer Co was going to store product in fixed positions, it would have to plan around a minimum of 7,600 cubic feet of actual storage space. Although each of these items is required to produce Hammer Company's products, they are not all needed at the same time. On average Hammer only has on hand 30 percent of any of the above items at any one time. If it used a random locator system it would plan for approximately 2,280 cubic feet of actual storage area.

COMBINATION SYSTEMS

A system that blends many of the best features of fixed and random locator systems are combination systems.

Basic Concept

Combination systems enable you to assign specific locations to those items requiring special consideration, while the bulk of the product mix will be randomly located. Very few systems are purely fixed or purely random.

Conceptually, you are trying to enjoy the best features of the fixed and random systems. You achieve this by assigning only selected items to fixed homes—but not all items. Therefore, you only have to plan around the maximum space required by the selected items instead of that required by all items. For the items not in fixed homes, you can plan around the average quantities you expect to have on a daily, ongoing basis. So, the fixed system is used for the selected items and the random system for everything else.

A common application of the combination system approach is where certain items are an organization's primary product or raw materials line and must be placed as close as possible to a packing/shipping area or to a manufacturing workstation. Those items are assigned a fixed position, while the remainder of the product line is randomly positioned elsewhere. See Exhibit 3–8 for typical scenarios for utilizing a combination locator system.

Common Item Placement Theories

Locator systems provide a broad overview of where SKUs will be found within a facility. Physical control of inventory is enhanced by narrowing the focus of how product should be laid out within any particular location system. As with locator systems, item place-

Exhibit 3–8 Typical Scenarios Involving Combination Location Systems

Scenario One: Barash Foods decided to speed up its order filling efforts by changing where product was located in relationship to the shipping dock. First it determined which 15–20 percent of its product lines showed up on 80 percent of its orders. These items would be assigned to fixed positions close to the point-of-use (shipping dock), while those items found in only 20 percent of the orders would be randomly stored.

Barash had to decide if these fixed homes would be large enough to hold 100 percent of the cubic space necessary to house a product if the maximum quantity of it was in the facility at one time during the year. The company decided it could not devote that much space per product in the limited area closest to the point-of-use. It therefore decided to allow for 100 percent of the space needed for one week's worth of product movement for the fixed location SKUs. In other words, while still having to follow the fixed location system rule that space must exist for 100 percent of the cubic space required for the maximum quantity of an item expected during a given time period, it controlled the space and quantity by shortening the timeframe.

Random items were stored in accordance with the general rule that random space is planned around the average quantity expected in an area during a defined time period. In this case the time period was one year.

Scenario Two: Charmax Manufacturing is a "job shop" electronics manufacturer. It manufactures special-order items and often will only produce one, never-to-be-repeated run of an item. Therefore, some specific raw materials inventories required for any given production run may never be needed in the future. However, the company uses many common electronics components such as resisters, transistors, and solder in most of the final assemblies it produces. Its physical plant is very small.

Charmax carefully reviews its master production schedule to determine when various subassemblies and final assemblies will be produced. It then analyzes the bill-of-materials (the recipe of components) for the sub- or final assemblies, and orders as much specific purpose items as possible on a to-be-delivered just-in-time basis. This holds down the quantity of nonstandard inventory it will have in-house at any one time.

Charmax then establishes fixed positions for working stock, both special-order and standard stock items, during a production cycle around the appropriate workstations. Where working stock would consume too much space around a work area, working reserve stock is placed in zone locations close to the workstations. Regular, general-use product, such as resisters and transistors, is stored in random order. This combination location system—which is comprised of fixed, zone, and random storage for working, working reserve, and general stock—allows Charmax to maximize its use of space at any given time.

ment theories (where should a particular item or category of items be physically positioned) go by many different names in trade literature. By whatever name, most approaches fall into one of three concepts: inventory stratification, family grouping, and special considerations.

INVENTORY STRATIFICATION

Inventory stratification consists of two parts:
1. A-B-C categorization of SKUs
2. Utilizing an SKU's unloading/loading ratio

A-B-C Categorization of SKUs

This item placement approach is based on "Pareto's Law." In 1907, an Italian sociologist and economist by the name of Vilfredo Pareto (1848–1923) expressed his belief that 80 to 85 percent of Italy's money was held by only 15 to 20 percent of the country's population. He called the small, wealthy group the "vital few" and everyone else the "trivial many." This ultimately came to be known as the "80–20 Rule," or Pareto's Law. The concept stands for the proposition that within any given population of things, approximately 20 percent of them have 80 percent of the "value" of all of the items concentrated within them, and that the other 80 percent only have 20 percent of the value concentrated within them. "Value" can be defined in various ways. For example, if the criterion is money, then 20 percent of all items represent 80 percent of the dollar value of all items. If the criterion is usage rate, then 20 percent of all items represent the 80 percent of the items most often used/sold.

Accordingly, for efficient physical inventory control, using popularity (speed of movement into and through the facility) as the criterion, the most productive overall location for an item is a storage position closest to that item's point-of-use. SKUs are separated into A-B-C categories, with "A" representing the most popular, fastest moving items (the "vital few"), "B" representing the next most active, and "C" the slow movers.

Providing product to outside customers is often the chief objective of a distribution environment. Therefore, in a distribution environment, the point-of-use would be the shipping dock. In a manufacturing environment, a workstation would become the point-of-use, with the most active, most often required raw materials positioned in near proximity to it.

To separate an inventory into A-B-C categories, create a sorted matrix that presents all SKUs in descending order of importance and allows for the calculation of those items representing the greatest concentration of value. Exhibit 3–9 represents selected rows of a complete listing of SKUs.

What the Matrix Shows

Before attempting to understand how the matrix is mathematically constructed, you first have to explore what information the matrix is presenting. Unless otherwise stated, all references are to Exhibit 3–9.

▸ Column A is merely a sequential listing of the number of SKUs in the total population. The example shows 300 items. If an organization had 2,300 SKUs, Column A of its matrix would end with Row 2,300.

▸ Recall that Pareto's Law has two components. The first refers to the percentage of all items that a certain number of items represent, and the second to the percentage value that the same grouping of items has when compared to the value of all other items combined.

▸ Column G reflects the first aspect. For example, 30 items represent 10 percent of 300. Therefore, Column G, Row 30 shows 10 percent of all 300 items.

▸ Column F reflects the second aspect. For example, the first three items (Rows 1, 2, and 3) of Column A have a combined value (usage rate) of 15.5 percent. That 15.5 percent

Exhibit 3–9 Categorization for Item Placement by Popularity

A	B	C	D	E	F	G
Line No.	Part No.	Description	Annual Usage	Cumulative Usage	% Total Usage	% Total Items
I	Part 79	Product A	8,673	8,673.00	6.3%	0.3%
2	Part 133	Product B	6,970	15,643.00	11.3%	0.7%
3	Part 290	Product C	5,788	21,431.00	15.5%	1.0%
.						
.						
.						
17	Part 70	Product Q	1,896	64,915.00	47.0%	5.7%
18	Part 117	Product R	1,888	66,803.00	48.4%	6.0%
19	Part 134	Product S	1,872	68,675.00	49.7%	6.3%
20	Part 170	Product T	1,687	70,362.00	50.9%	6.7%
21	Part 182	Product U	1,666	72,028.00	52.1%	7.0%
22	Part 28	Product V	1,646	73,674.00	53.3%	7.3%
.						
.						
.						
30	Part 278	Product AD	997	82,919.00	60.0%	10.0%
.						
.						
.						
93	Part 295	Product CJ	325	123,350.00	89.3%	31.0%
94	Part 30	Product CK	325	123,675.00	89.5%	31.3%
95	Part 11	Product CL	323	123,998.00	89.8%	31.7%
96	Part 192	Product CM	321	124,319.00	90.0%	32.0%
97	Part 96	Product CN	321	124,640.00	90.2%	32.3%
98	Part 40	Product CO	298	124,938.00	90.4%	32.7%
.						
.						
.						
272	Part 86	Product JG	6	138,053.00	99.9%	90.7%
273	Part 32	Product JH	6	138,059.00	99.9%	91.0%
274	Part 129	Product JI	5	138,064.00	99.9%	91.3%
275	Part 164	Product JJ	5	138,069.00	100.0%	91.7%
276	Part 283	Product JK	5	138,074.00	100.0%	92.0%
277	Part 252	Product JL	5	138,079.00	100.0%	92.3%
.						
.						
.						
298	Part 151	Product KG	—	138,134.00	100.0%	99.3%
299	Part 61	Product KH	—	138,134.00	100.0%	99.7%
300	Part 165	Product KI	—	138,134.00	100.0%	100.0%

is shown at Row 3 of Column F. (How the 15.5 percent is arrived at is explained below in "Creating the Matrix.")

▸ After creating the matrix, a review of Column F leads to decisions as to where the cutoff should be for each (A-B-C) category. There is no rule of thumb. The decision is a common sense, intuitive one. In Exhibit 3–9, since 19 of all items represented almost 50 percent of the value of all items (see Row 19, Column F), it seems appropriate to cut off the A category at that number. It would have been just as appropriate to cut it off at Row 20, Column F, which shows 50.9 percent.

Creating the Matrix

Here is how to create the matrix:

▸ Most application software programs include a report generator module that allows various fields of information, such as SKU identifiers, descriptions, and quantities, to be extracted from the general database and saved in a generically formatted (ASCII) file.[1] This information may then be exported into one of the commonly available spreadsheet software programs such as Excel. Rather than undertaking the data entry required to input the information found in Columns B, C, and D, you should obtain this information from your report generator and then export it into a spreadsheet program.

▸ Column A—reflects the number of SKUs being analyzed. It is organized in ascending numeric sequence (1, 2, 3 ...).

▸ Column B—SKU number/identifier.

▸ Column C—SKU description.

▸ Column D—Annual usage quantity of the SKU.

In a retail/distribution environment, where the inventory is comprised of finished goods, Column D will contain the immediately preceding 12 months' usage quantities. This is based on the rule of thumb that the product lines will remain relatively unchanged during the upcoming 12-month period. The immediately preceding 12 months' usage rates will reflect any product trends and is more timely than using the immediate past calendar year's rates.

In a manufacturing environment, raw materials, components, and subassemblies used during the past 12 months may not be required during the upcoming 12 months. Therefore, the data for Column D must be derived from the master production schedule (the projection of what is to be built and in what quantities). After determining what will be built and in what quantities, examine the bill-of-materials (BOM), the recipe of what pieces and parts will actually go into the items to be manufactured. The data necessary for Column D is ascertained by multiplying the appropriate items in the BOM times the quantity of items to be built.

Column D is sorted in descending order, with the highest use item appearing at the top and the most inactive item at the bottom.

Column D is the sort field. However, if only Column D was sorted, the information in it would become disassociated from the SKUs the data represents, which information is reflected in Columns B and C. Therefore, the sort range includes columns B, C, and D so that all related information is sorted together.

▶ E—Cumulative total of Column D.

To derive the percentage value that a number of items have compared to the value of all items, it is necessary to establish that overall value as well as the value that any given number of items added together may possess. This is what Column E does.

Note that the first row of Column E is the same as the first row of Column D. Note that adding together the first two rows of Column D results in the second row of Column E. The sum of the first three rows of Column D equals the third row of Column E. The sum of the first 17 rows of Column D results in the data in Row 17 of Column E, and so forth.

The data shown in Row 300 of Column E reflects the usage value of all 300 items added together. The information on any given Row of Column E reflects the value of all of the preceding SKUs added to the value of that specific row's value.

▶ F—This is the second aspect of Pareto's Law. It reflects the percentage value that a grouping of items has when compared to the value of all other items.

Column F is derived by dividing every row of Column E by the last value of Column E. In other words, the first value in Column F (6.3 percent) results from dividing the first row of Column E (8,673) by the last row of Column E (138,134). The value found in Row 2 of Column F is derived from dividing the amount shown in Row 2 of Column E (15,643) by the last row of Column E (138,134), and so forth. Using arithmetic terminology, each row of Column E acts as a numerator, the last row of Column E is the denominator, and the quotient is found in Column F.

▶ G—This is the first aspect of Pareto's Law. It reflects the percentage of all items compared with all other items. In other words, 3 is 1 percent of 300.

▶ Column G is derived by dividing every row of Column A by the last number in Column A. In other words, the first value in Column G (0.3 percent) results from dividing the first row of Column A (1) by the last row of Column A (300). The value found in Row 2 of Column G is derived from dividing the amount shown in Row 2 of Column A (2) by the last row of Column A (300), and so forth.

▶ After creating the chart, you look down Columns F and G
and decide where you want to place the cutoff for categories
A, B, and C. Product would then be arranged according to
its category.

▶ Appendix B sets out the formulae necessary to create the
matrix for 300 SKUs in Microsoft Excel®.

Utilizing an SKU's Unloading/Loading Ratio

Even more efficiency in physical inventory control can be achieved
through placing items within the A-B-C zones according to that
SKU's unloading-to-loading ("unloading/loading") ratio. The un-
loading/loading ratio reflects the number of trips necessary to
bring an item to a storage location compared with the number of
trips required to transport it from a storage point to a point-of-
use. If one trip was required to bring in and store a case of product,
but 10 trips were required to actually take its contents to a point-
of-use, the unloading/loading ratio would be 1 to 10 (1:10). Sub-
stantial reductions in handling times can be achieved through
application of this principle. See Exhibit 3–10.

The closer the unloading/loading ratio is to 1:1, the less it mat-
ters where an item is stored within an A-B-C zone because the
travel time is the same on either side of the storage location. The
more the ratio increases, the more critical it is to place an item
closer to its point-of-use. Assuming 7 productive hours of labor
within an 8-hour work shift, a reduction of even 30 seconds in
travel time every 5 minutes will result in a time savings of 42 minutes. See Exhibit 3–11.

FAMILY GROUPING

An alternative to the A-B-C approach is the family grouping/like product approach. This approach to item placement positions items with

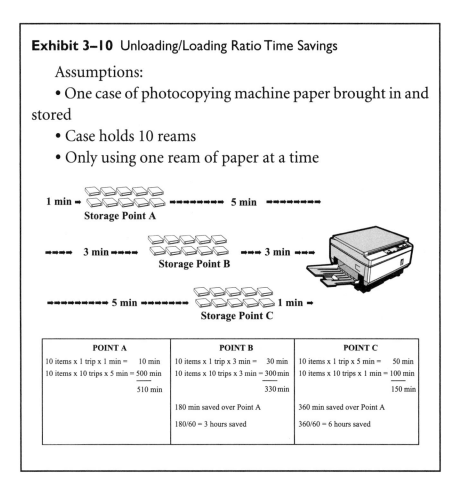

Exhibit 3–10 Unloading/Loading Ratio Time Savings

Assumptions:
• One case of photocopying machine paper brought in and stored
• Case holds 10 reams
• Only using one ream of paper at a time

1 min → Storage Point A → 5 min →

→ 3 min → Storage Point B → 3 min →

→ 5 min → Storage Point C 1 min →

POINT A	POINT B	POINT C
10 items x 1 trip x 1 min = 10 min	10 items x 1 trip x 3 min = 30 min	10 items x 1 trip x 5 min = 50 min
10 items x 10 trips x 5 min = 500 min	10 items x 10 trips x 3 min = 300 min	10 items x 10 trips x 1 min = 100 min
510 min	330 min	150 min
	180 min saved over Point A	360 min saved over Point A
	180/60 = 3 hours saved	360/60 = 6 hours saved

similar characteristics together. Theoretically, similar characteristics will lead to a natural grouping of items, which will be received/stored/picked/shipped together.

Groupings can be based on:

▸ Like characteristics—widgets with widgets, gidgits with gidgits, gadgets with gadgets.

▸ Items that are regularly sold together—parts needed to tune up a car.

Exhibit 3–11 Practical Effect of Inventory Layout Changes

If a change in procedure, layout, product design, paper-work, or any other factor saved 30 seconds every 5 minutes, how much time would you save each day?

- Assume 7 actual work hours per day
- 60 minutes × 7 hours = 420 minutes
- 420 minutes ÷ 5 minutes = 84 segments
- 84 × 30 seconds = 2,560 seconds
- 2,560 seconds ÷ 60 seconds = 42 minutes

Saving 30 seconds every 5 minutes saves 42 minutes per day!

▶ Items that are regularly used together—strap with sports goggles.

Pros

There are a number of advantages to using family groups, including:

▶ Ease of storage and retrieval using similar techniques and equipment.

▶ Ease of recognition of product groupings.

▶ Ease of using zoning location systems.

Cons

Before using the family grouping approach you should carefully consider some of its negatives, as follows:

▶ Some items are so similar they become substituted one for the other, such as electronics parts.

▶ Danger of properly positioning an active item close to its point-of-use, but consuming valuable space close to that area by housing far less active "family member" items with their popular relative.

▶ Danger of housing an active product with its inactive relatives far from the popular SKU's point-of-use, all for the sake of keeping like items together.

▶ An item can be used in more than one family.

▶ Using inventory stratification and family grouping together

Effective item placement can often be achieved through tying both the inventory stratification and family grouping approaches together. For example, assume order-filling personnel travel up and down a main travel aisle, moving into picking aisles to select items, and then back out to the main aisle to proceed further. Further, assume 12 brands of Gidgits are all stored in the same area for purposes of family grouping. Pareto's Law indicates that not all brands of Gidgits will be equally popular. Consequently, using both the inventory stratification and family grouping concepts together, the most popular Gidgit brands are positioned closer to the main travel aisle and the least popular furthest from it. The end result is a more efficient overall layout.

SPECIAL CONSIDERATIONS

A product's characteristics may force us to receive/store/pick/ship it in a particular manner. The product may be extremely heavy or light, toxic or flammable, frozen, odd in shape, and so on.

Even with items requiring special handling or storage, such as frozen food stored in a freezer, the inventory stratification and family grouping concepts can and should be employed to ensure efficient inventory layout.

Location Addresses and SKU Identifiers

You simply cannot control what you can't find. Therefore, it is imperative that you create and maintain a system of location addresses and SKU identifiers. Those two elements are essential to tracking an item no matter where it goes.

SIGNIFICANCE

Major contributing factors to the success of inventory systems are:

▶ Adequate, appropriate identification markings on SKUs, including both SKU number and stock keeping unit of measure. These markings allow a worker to quickly and easily identify an item without having to read and translate product descriptions and confusing pack size designations. This ease of recognition reduces errors and the time required for either stock selection or put-away.

▶ Adequate, appropriate identification markings on bin/slot/floor/rack/drawer/shelf locations. Just like the address on a house, the address of a specific location in the stockroom lets you quickly find the "tenant" or "homeowner" SKU you are looking for.

▶ Procedures tying any given SKU to the location it is in at any given time. How does the post office know where to send mail to someone who has moved? Obviously, the relocated person fills out a change of address form. In much the same manner, you must set up a procedure that tells your system where a product lives, and if it moves—where to.

▶ Procedures tying a single SKU to multiple locations in which it is stored. If you have two homes, you let your friends know the addresses. Your friends then put that information together in their address books. You must do the same thing for products residing in two or more locations within the building.

▶ A system for tracking items, on a timely basis, as they change locations. Whatever form your "change of address" form takes, it has to be filled out and processed quickly.

▶ Package advertising that does not obscure SKU identifier codes.

▶ Use of simple marking systems that are easy to read and understand. You should avoid complicated marking systems that are difficult to read, understand, recall, or are conducive to numerical transposition. For example, markings such as "2/24 oz" and "24/12 oz" are quantity-oriented coding employing numbers describing the quantity and size of the inner packages. However, such numbers are easily reversed or transposed, and are not intuitively understood.

If you incorporate these elements into your inventory systems, you can expect:

▶ Decreased labor costs related to search time for product. These search-time savings manifest themselves not only when you search for an individual item, but most definitely when product is located in multiple unspecified locations.

▶ Decreased labor costs associated with searching for appropriate storage locations.

▶ Elimination of the unnecessary purchase of items that are already in the facility but are undiscovered when needed.

▶ Correct selection of SKUs during order filling.

▶ Correct selection of pack size(s) during order fulfillment.

All of the above lead to more accurate inventory tracking, less wasted time to correct errors, and an increase in customer satisfaction.

KEYS TO EFFECTIVELY TYING TOGETHER SKUs AND LOCATION ADDRESSES

To keep track of where SKUs are at any given time, it is necessary to:

- ▶ Clearly mark items with an SKU identifier.
- ▶ Clearly mark items with a unit of measure such as pack size.
- ▶ Clearly mark location addresses on bins/slots/shelves/racks/floor locations/drawers/and so on.
- ▶ Tie SKU numbers and location addresses together either in a manual card file system or within a computerized database.
- ▶ Update product moves on a real-time basis with bar coding coupled with radio frequency scanners (see Chapter 4, "Automatic Identification").

Clearly Mark Items with an SKU Identifier; Clearly Mark Items with a Unit of Measure

Too often, managers believe that workers can read and understand a product's markings and packaging. The end result of this belief is error after error. To eliminate many of these identification miscues, you need to clearly mark items with an identifying number and a unit of measure. Workers will make far fewer errors matching a number on a box to the same number on a piece of paper than they will trying to match words or abbreviated descriptions.

The SKU identifier is generally an organization's own internal identifying code for the item, rather than a manufacturer's or customer's number for that SKU. Although the SKU number itself is often adequate for identification purposes, in manufacturing it may be necessary to also include lot and serial numbers to aid in quality control. Lot and serial numbers make it possible to track manufacturing batch, date, location, and inspector. Exhibit 3–12 reflects various methods of getting items actually labeled or marked.

Markings related to unit of measure (such as each/pair/dozen/barrel/ounce/pound/cylinder/barrel/case) also serve to greatly reduce error in picking and shipping.

Exhibit 3–12 Marking SKUs

By manufacturer

• Manufacturer prints or affixes plain, human readable label on the item and/or a bar code label with coding on the items. Manufacturer obtains labels or you provide them.

At vendor site

• Vendor from whom you obtain the product prints or affixes your plain, human readable label on the item and/or a bar code label with coding on the items. Manufacturer obtains labels or you provide them.

At time of receiving

• Everything comes through receiving—it is a natural node. That convergence allows you the opportunity to affix plain, human readable label on the item and/or a bar code label with coding on the items.

• You can have all product that turns even once during the year marked in this manner, with faster moving items (12 turns a year) all marked within a few weeks.

Clearly Mark Location Addresses on Bins/Slots/Shelves/Racks/Floor Locations/Drawers

Just as you could not find a house in a city if its address was not clearly identified, you cannot find a storage location unless its address is clearly marked or easily discerned in some other manner. The addressing or location system you choose should have an underlying logic that is easy to understand. Addresses should be as short as possible, yet they should convey all needed information.

You should first consider whether the system will be all numeric, all alphabetic (alpha), or alpha-numeric. In deciding which system to adopt, consider the following:

▸ All numeric systems require sufficient digit positions to allow for future growth. Because each numeric position only allows for 10 variations (0–9), numeric systems sometimes become too lengthy. In other words, since a single numeric position only allows 10 variations, if you required 100 different variations (for 100 different SKUs), you would need two digit positions, representing 00 through 99 (10 × 10). One thousand variations would require three numeric positions, 000 through 999, and so on. See Exhibit 3–13, Alpha-Numeric Variations.

Exhibit 3–13 Alpha-Numeric Variations

0 → 9 = 10	
00 → 99 = 100	10 × 10 = 100
000 → 999 = 1,000	10 × 10 × 10 = 1,000
A → Z = 26	
AA → ZZ = 676	26 × 26 = 676
AAA → ZZZ = 17,576	26 × 26 × 26 = 17,576

▶ Systems that are completely alphabetic allow for 26 variations per position, A through Z (assuming only capital letters). Two alphas together, AA through ZZ (26 × 26), allow for 676 variations. Three alphas, AAA through ZZZ, allow for 17,576 variations. See Exhibit 3–13, Alpha-Numeric Variations. Although alphas provide numerous variations in a short address, systems that are completely alphabetic are visually confusing (HFZP).

▶ Alpha-numeric systems often provide for visual differentiation while allowing sufficient variations in a short address.

▶ *Caution*: While alpha systems require fewer characters to hold the same number of variations, they are more error prone. For example: Is that the number zero or the letter O? A one or the letter l? A two or the letter Z? A P or an R? A Q or an O? If you are only dealing with a computer system, then characters are "cheap," and you could use only numerics to avoid confusion. However, if part of your system will involve human-readable labels, placards, or markings where a long string of numbers might present a problem or where you are trying to keep a bar code label short, you might have to balance out the merits of shorter alpha-numeric systems against longer pure numeric systems.

Exhibit 3–14 presents some common location addressing systems for racks or shelving. Exhibit 3–15 presents common location addressing systems for bulk storage.

Exhibit 3–14 Addressing Racks, Drawers, and Shelving

APPROACH	EXPLANATION
"Street Address" 03A02B02	03 A 02 B 02 Room Aisle Rack Tier Slot (City) (Street) (Building) (Floor) (Apt.) Although this is a lengthy address if an automated storage and retrieval system (AS/RS) is used, detailed exact spot information is required for the selector arm to find the desired load.
"Rack-Section-Tier-Bin" 030342	03 03 4 2 Rack Section* Tier Bin *A rack section is that portion of the weight bearing horizontal support between two upright supports.
Room/Bldg-Rack-Bin AA001	A A 001 Rm/Bldg Rack Bin
Rack-Bin AA001	AA 001 Rack Bin These last two systems are short, simple, and easy to remember, but they do not provide tier information.

Tie SKU Numbers and Location Addresses Together

The placement of identifiers on both product and physical locations creates an infrastructure by which you can track product as it moves. The next step is marrying together an SKU number and the location(s) where that item is located. This can be easily accomplished by using a simple 3 × 5 card file system (which should be computerized as soon as possible). See Exhibit 3–16.

Exhibit 3–15 Bulk Storage Grid Addressing System

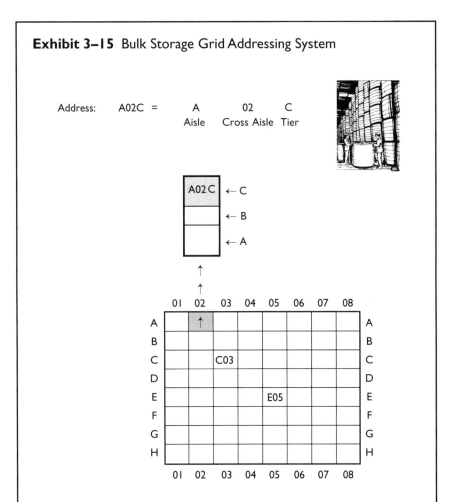

Address: A02C =   A   02   C
                    Aisle Cross Aisle Tier

• In bulk storage areas, you can utilize a simple grid denoted with placards on walls or on the building's structural supports to find an address on the floor. This is done through two lines bisecting on a flat plain.

• For vertical addresses, you triangulate three lines.

• The above is applied geometry (Cartesian Coordinates) developed by René Descartes, the famous French mathematician.

Exhibit 3–16 Simple Card File Tracking System

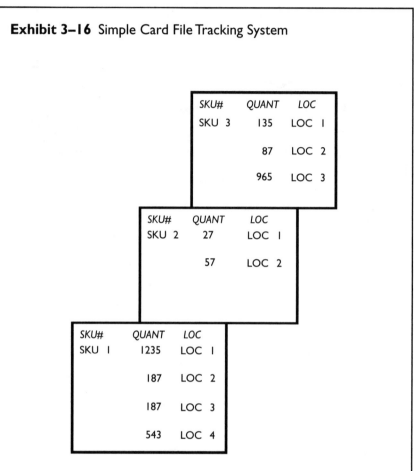

SKU#	QUANT	LOC
SKU 3	135	LOC 1
	87	LOC 2
	965	LOC 3

SKU#	QUANT	LOC
SKU 2	27	LOC 1
	57	LOC 2

SKU#	QUANT	LOC
SKU 1	1235	LOC 1
	187	LOC 2
	187	LOC 3
	543	LOC 4

Cards are marked with all SKU numbers. Cards will be indexed in ascending number sequence—lowest SKU number in the front of the file box and the highest SKU number appearing last. All locations and quantities for that specific item are noted. As SKUs are added-to or moved, card file information is updated as often as possible. Updates should occur at least twice daily, for example, during the lunch hour and at the end of the workday.

Update Product Moves

A final step in managing inventory is tracking it as it is added to, deleted, or moved. This challenge exists for any organization whether or not the company uses manual tracking, computerized approaches, or bar coding.

The best generally available approach for real-time tracking of items as they move is using bar coding mobile scanners with radio frequency (RF) capability. See Chapter 4, "Automatic Identification."

If RF-capable bar coding is not available, then updating can be accomplished as follows:

▸ Portable bar code scanners that capture the information within the scanner mechanism or on a disk in the scanner. The information is then uploaded into the computerized database either through the communications ports on the scanner and computer, or by loading the scanner disk into the computer.

▸ Manually captured, paper-based information (see Exhibit 3-17) is entered into the database through keying (data entry by a human being).

▸ Manually captured, paper-based information is manually written onto file cards.

Exhibit 3–17 Bulk Storage Grid Addressing System

STOCK MOVEMENT REPORT

SKU# _____

Date _____   Time _____

Quantity _____

From _____   To _____

▶ No matter what method is used, it is imperative that information relative to inventory additions, deletions, or movement be inputted into the system as soon as possible. To the greatest extent possible, the shelf count (what is actually in the facility and where it is) should match the record count (the amount reflected in the main database records). The longer the time lag between inventory movement and information capture and updating of the record count, the greater the chance for error, lost product, and increased costs.

Recap

Organizations should carefully consider specific item placement within an overall location system to maximize each SKU's accessibility while being mindful of that item's point-of-use, unloading/loading ratio, relationship to similar items, or characteristics requiring special handling.

Organizations lacking procedures that identify the location of each SKU within the facility suffer from excessive labor costs, "lost" product causing additional items to be purchased to cover for those on-site but unavailable when required, poor customer service, and general confusion. Controlling product location and movement centers around establishing an overall locator system that effectively reflects the organization's basic inventory nature such as finished goods in a retail/distribution environment or raw materials and subassemblies in a manufacturing facility. Often legitimate operational and storage objectives are in conflict with one another, resulting in final location system decisions made on the basis of a series of tradeoffs.

And finally, each item's present location must be identified with that SKU's identifier, with address and quantity changes being updated on an ongoing, timely basis.

REVIEW QUESTIONS

1. Honeycombing is best described as:
   (a) product unevenly stacked.
   (b) matrix racking or shelving layout.
   (c) empty space in usable storage areas.
   (d) the number of items per level and the number of tiers of product on a pallet.

2. Memory location systems:
   (a) are simple and efficient.
   (b) are human dependent.
   (c) require updating of location information.
   (d) are useful when a large number of different SKUs must be quickly located.

3. Regarding random locator systems:
   (a) each item has an assigned home in a random zone.
   (b) an item's home is the location it is in while it is there.
   (c) an SKU's storage location must be planned around the maximum quantity of that item expected to be on-site during a defined time period.
   (d) only certain items may be placed in the bulk storage areas of the facility.

4. In relationship to its unloading/loading ratio, an SKU should be placed closer to its point of use if the ratio is:
   (a) 1:28.

(b) 1:1.

(c) 3:15.

(d) 28:28.

5. Pareto's Law holds that:

   (a) 80 percent of all items account for 80 percent of the dollar value of 20 percent of those items.

   (b) 20 percent of all items account for 20 percent of the usage value of 80 percent of those items.

   (c) 80 percent of all items contain 20 percent of the value of those items.

   (d) a fixed locator system is operationally efficient 20 percent of the time for 80 percent of all items.

Answers

1. (c), 2. (b), 3. (b), 4. (a), 5. (c)

Note

1. American Standard Code of Information Interchange (ASCII) is the basic 128-character set understood by all computer systems.

CHAPTER 4

AUTOMATIC IDENTIFICATION

Errors and time increase dramatically the more often a human being is involved in identifying an object, inputting that information into a database, and then modifying the knowledge to keep track of changes in location, pack size, quantity, and so on.

The less you rely on human intervention to identify items, input information, and track data, the more timely and accurate your records will be.

Automatic Identification (*Auto ID*) refers to a broad range of technologies that are used to help machines identify objects without the need for a human being to key in the information. Auto ID is often coupled with automatic data capture. These technologies include bar codes, smart cards, voice recognition, some biometric technologies (retinal scans, for instance), optical character recognition, and radio-frequency identification (RFID). One-dimensional, linear bar coding is the most common method of automated inventory identification. In recent years, stacked symbologies, often called "2D symbologies" consisting of a given linear symbology repeated vertically in multiple and presented in various shapes, have evolved. Given the large number of 2D symbologies and their rapidly changing properties, this chapter will only deal with one-dimensional, linear bar coding—and with RFID.

The Basics of Bar Coding

Bar coding, an optical method of achieving automatic identification, is a major tool in capturing critical data quickly and accurately. It relies on visible or invisible light being reflected off of a printed pattern. The dark bars or dark areas within the pattern absorb light, and the intervening spaces or areas reflect light. The contrasting absorption and reflection is sensed by a device that "reads" this reflected pattern and decodes the information.

The time and dollar savings that would be realized if your organization could eliminate the time and errors noted above will often pay for a bar coding system. The speed of information capture and the accuracy of bar coding are often sufficient reasons to cost-justify installing bar coding within your operation.

Bar coding is not the only automated method of identifying inventory. For example, there is also optical character reading, machine vision, magnetic stripe, surface acoustic wave, and radio-frequency tags. See Exhibit 4–1.

Bar code systems generally consist of three components: the code itself, the reading device(s), and the printer(s). The objective of this chapter is to provide you with a working knowledge of (1) elements of a bar code symbol; (2) the fundamentals of the more commonly used linear bar code languages/symbologies in the inventory control world; (3) printing and scanning (reading) basics; and (4) some practical bar code applications.

Elements of a Bar Code Symbol

Why can you easily read the sentence, "Inventory control is fun?" You can read that sentence because you recognize the alphabet and understand the rules of grammar and sentence construction. A bar code "symbology" or language is very similar because it has a fixed

Exhibit 4–1 Various Automated Methods of Identifying Inventory

Technology	How It Works	For Your Information
Optical Character Reading (OCR)	Numbers, letters, and characters are printed in a predetermined, standard character style or font. Like a bar code, the image is illuminated and the reflection is sensed and decoded.	• Allows for both human and machine readability • 10 characters per inch data density • Slower read rate than bar codes • Higher error rate than bar codes • Very sensitive to print quality
Machine Vision	Cameras take pictures of objects, encode, and send them to a computer for interpretation.	• Very accurate under the right light conditions • Reads at moderate speed • Expensive
Magnetic Stripe	A magnetic stripe, like those on credit cards, is encoded with information.	• Proven technology • Readable through grease and dirt • Relatively high density of information—25 to 70 characters per inch • Information can be changed • Must use a contact reader, making high-speed reading of many items impractical • Not human readable
Surface Acoustic Wave (SAW)	Data is encoded on a chip that is encased in a tag. In response to a radar pulse from a reader with a special antenna, the tag converts the pulse to an ultrasonic acoustic wave. Each tag is uniquely programmed so that the resulting acoustic wave has an amplitude matching the chip's code. The wave is converted back to an electromagnetic signal sent back to the reader.	• Can be used in highly hazardous environments such as high heat and acid baths • Can be read up to 6 feet away • No line of sight required • Physically durable
Radio-Frequency Tag	Data is encoded on a chip that is encased in a tag. In response to a radar pulse from a reader with a special antenna, a transponder in the tag sends a signal to the reader.	• Tags can be programmable or permanently coded • Can be read up to 30 feet away • No line of sight required • Physically durable—life in excess of 10 years

alphabet made up of various patterns of dark bars and intervening light spaces coupled with rules for how it is presented.

There are many types of bar codes, not all of which consist of the linear symbols most commonly found in the inventory control world. For example:

Appearance of common one-dimensional, linear types of bar code patterns:

Appearance of common two-dimensional, matrix and stacked bar code patterns:

Presently, linear bar codes are the most commonly used for general inventory control purposes.

Structure of a
Generic Bar Code Symbol

The entire pattern is called the "symbol." Each bar or space is called an "element."

QUIET ZONE

Symbols can be read from left to right or right to left. A bar code scanner (reader) must make a number of measurements to decode the symbol accurately. The quiet zones on each side of the symbol gives the scanner a starting point from which to start its measurement.

START AND STOP CHARACTERS

For codes to be read from either direction or top to bottom or bottom to top in a vertically oriented symbol, start and stop characters tell the scanner where the message begins. It is customary for the character on the left or at the top of the symbol to be the start character, and the one on the right or bottom to be the stop character.

DATA CHARACTERS

The data characters are the actual message within the code. These can be letters of the alphabet, numbers, symbols (+, −, /, =), or a combination of all three.

"X" DIMENSION

The narrowest bar or space in a bar code is called the "X" dimension. This width can run from 5 mils to 50 mils. A mil is one-thousandth of an inch.

This width is very important because it determines how wide

each narrow and wide bar or space will be. The narrow bars/spaces are a single "X" in width, while the wide bars/spaces can be two, three, or four "Xs" wide. Therefore, an element (a bar or space) can be a single "X" or several "Xs."

The larger the "X" dimension of a symbol, the easier it is to read.

Symbologies: Bar Coding Structural Rules

Just as there are rules for how an English sentence is structured, for the relationship of upper-case to lower-case letters, and for punctuation, similar rules govern bar codes. These rules are set out in a "symbology." A symbology controls how information will be encoded in a bar code symbol.

Just as there are different languages, such as French, English, Spanish, Italian, Russian, Japanese, and Chinese, there are different symbologies. Common symbologies found in the inventory world are Code 39, Code 128, Interleaved 2 of 5, and UPC.

Symbologies are like typefaces with different character sets and separate printing characteristics. Some symbologies only present numbers. Some have numbers, upper-case alphabetics (A–Z), and limited special characters. Others have both upper- and lower-case alphabetics (A–Z, a–z), numbers, and a wide range of special characters. Some symbologies only allow for a set number of characters in a pattern, while others allow for variable-length messages.

DISCRETE AND CONTINUOUS SYMBOLOGIES

Bar codes can either be discrete or continuous. Characters in a discrete code start with a bar and end with a bar, and they have a space between each character. Characters in a continuous code start with a bar, end with a space, and have no gap between one character and another. The primary significance of the difference is that a discrete code is easier to print and read, but you can get more characters per inch with a continuous code.

Which of the following is easier to read?

Symbologies Symbologies Symbologies Symbologies

The word on the far left is the most difficult to read but has the greatest amount of information in the smallest amount of space, which is a good thing on a bar code label with limited space available. The word on the far right is the easiest to read, would allows for a more forgiving print job (for example, if the ink spread on the label surface between each letter, we would still be able to read it), but it takes up more space. Discrete symbologies are easier to print and read, but they take up more space.

SYMBOLOGY SUMMARY

The rules of a particular symbology control are:

▶ Character set—which alphabetics, numbers, and special characters are in the symbology?

▶ Symbology type—discrete or continuous? See Exhibit 4–2.

▶ Number of element widths—how many different "Xs" are there in the wide bars/spaces?

▶ Fixed or variable lengths of characters in a pattern?

▶ Density—how many characters can appear per inch?

POPULAR SYMBOLOGIES FOUND IN THE INVENTORY WORLD

Dozens of bar code symbologies exist. Many have failed in the marketplace because a large number of printer and scanner suppliers will not support them. Others are owned by individual companies

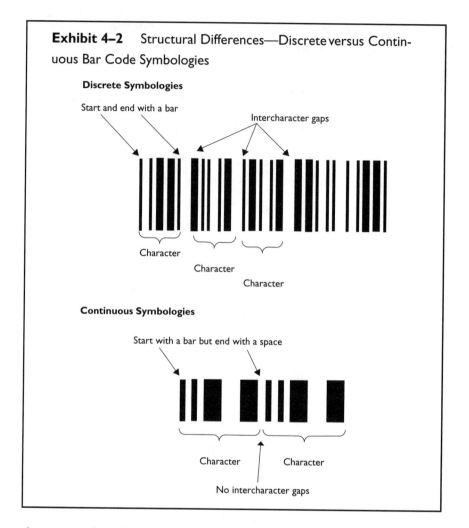

Exhibit 4–2 Structural Differences—Discrete versus Continuous Bar Code Symbologies

Discrete Symbologies

Start and end with a bar

Intercharacter gaps

Character

Character

Character

Continuous Symbologies

Start with a bar but end with a space

Character

Character

No intercharacter gaps

that control and limit their use. Others have specialized uses, such as Postnet, which is used by the U.S. Postal Service. Some are widely supported and accepted in the inventory control world.

Universal Product Code/European Article Numbering System

Without question, when dealing with point-of-sale identification of product (as in a grocery or other retail store), the bar code used is the Universal Product Code (UPC). A very similar code, which will eventually be interchangeable with UPC, is the European Article Numbering System (EAN).

The UPC symbology is highly structured and controlled, and it is only used in general merchandise retailing. It is an all numeric, fixed-length (11 characters) symbology. The UPC symbol is physically arranged into two halves. The left half has six numbers that identify the manufacturer or packager. The right half identifies the product. See Exhibit 4–3. You have to license the right to use the UPC from the Uniform Code Council (UCC), an organization created by the grocery industry.

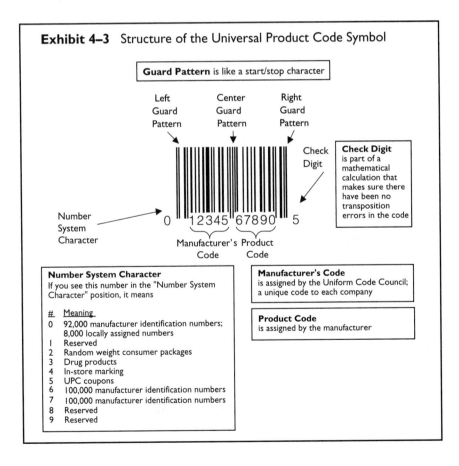

Exhibit 4–3 Structure of the Universal Product Code Symbol

Guard Pattern is like a start/stop character

Left Guard Pattern
Center Guard Pattern
Right Guard Pattern

Check Digit

Check Digit is part of a mathematical calculation that makes sure there have been no transposition errors in the code

Number System Character

0 12345 67890 5

Manufacturer's Code Product Code

Number System Character
If you see this number in the "Number System Character" position, it means

#	Meaning
0	92,000 manufacturer identification numbers; 8,000 locally assigned numbers
I	Reserved
2	Random weight consumer packages
3	Drug products
4	In-store marking
5	UPC coupons
6	100,000 manufacturer identification numbers
7	100,000 manufacturer identification numbers
8	Reserved
9	Reserved

Manufacturer's Code
is assigned by the Uniform Code Council; a unique code to each company

Product Code
is assigned by the manufacturer

The UPC is not suitable for inventory control use within a warehousing or manufacturing facility where there is a need for variable-length messages, alpha-numeric coding, flexible identification patterns, and so on.

Code 39

This symbology is the most widely used bar code in nonretail applications. It was first introduced in 1975.

Most stockkeepers will be able to find a Code 39 software to interface with their existing application software systems. In other words, you should be able to find a Code 39 bar code package that will allow you to continue to use your existing in-house software, numbering systems, and internal procedures.

Code 39 is sometimes referred to as "3 of 9 Code" because three of the nine elements (bars or spaces) making up a Code 39 character are wide and the other six are narrow.

Code 39 was the first alpha-numeric symbology developed. Among its most important features are:

▶ Entire alphabet in upper-case letters

▶ All numerics (e.g., 0 through 9)

▶ Seven special characters: −, ., *, $, /, +, %, and a character representing a blank space

▶ Discrete symbology

▶ Allows variable-length symbols

▶ Allows two messages to be decoded and transmitted as one ("concatenation")

▶ Can be printed in a wide variety of technologies

▶ Although there are only 43 data characters in the basic Code 39 set, by using certain characters as internal codes, it is possible to encode all 128 ASCII (American Code of

Information Interchange) characters used by computers. This feature is cumbersome and is not widely used.

▶ Self checking, which means a single printing defect cannot cause an error where one character is mistaken for another.

Code 128

This code, introduced in 1981, has many desirable features, such as:

▶ It uses three start codes to allow the encoding of all 128 ASCII characters without cumbersome procedures. Therefore, you can use the entire alphabet in both upper- and lower-case, all 10 numerics, and all special characters. Each printed character can have one of three meanings.

▶ There is high data density and continuous symbology that uses the least amount of label space for messages of six or more characters.

▶ Tests have shown this to be a highly readable code with high message integrity.

▶ Code 128 has become one of the two standard bar code symbologies used to identify the contents of corrugated boxes. (The other standard for corrugated shipping boxes is Interleaved 2 of 5 symbology.)

▶ Code 128 allows for concatenation.

Which Symbology Is Right for Your Organization?

Each symbology has its strengths and weaknesses. There is no one "right" bar code language that will fit every organization's needs.

A starting point in reviewing appropriate symbologies actually begins with your own industry. Has your industry selected a particular type of symbology? For example, the automotive industry has been using Code 39 since 1980. You can obtain guidance from trade associations in your industry segment.

The reason to start with a symbology accepted by your industry is that direct application software and hardware will have been written or created for the specific requirements of your business. It is the old question, "Why recreate the wheel?"

If no symbology dominates your industry, then the real questions become, What do you want the system to do for you? and How large is your budget?

Scanning Basics

Something has to read a bar code. That something is a scanner. These electrooptical devices include a means of illuminating the symbol and measuring reflected light.

A scanner projects a tiny spot of light that crosses the bar code symbol and then measures the exact width of the bars and spaces. The measurement is determined by the amount of reflectance off of the dark and light bars and spaces. Software in either the scanner or in a separate plug-in device then translates the visual (analog) signal into a digital one that a computer can understand and then decodes what symbology (language) it is reading and the message contained in the pattern.

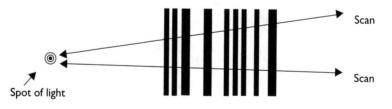

Light reflected is converted from an analog voltage (visual) format to a digital waveform for decoding.

The spot of light must not be larger than the "X" dimension

being used for that label or you will get misreads.

Scanner might believe that both
narrow bars are a single wide
element and that the space is
merely an ink void printing error.

Scanners must be purchased so that they match the "X" dimension that will be used for printing labels or for printing directly onto a surface.

Scanners can either be manual (where the user supplies the scanning motion) or automatic (where the device provides the scanning motion). See Exhibit 4–4.

PRINTING BASICS

Bar code printing can be done by the user on-site or by an off-site third-party vendor.

On-site printing generally occurs close to where product is either being received or shipped—its point-of-use.

Five basic on-site bar code print technologies are available: direct thermal, thermal transfer, dot matrix impact, ink jet, and laser (Xerographic). See Exhibit 4–5.

Off-site, commercial printers use a wide variety of printing techniques.

See Chapter 3, Exhibit 3–13, for a discussion of methods to affix bar code labels.

Bar Code Applications

It is far more important that you understand what you want to accomplish with bar codes than for you to understand all of the technical aspects of them.

Think of all of the bits and pieces of information you need to know to control inventory in a distribution environment. For example:

▶ Manufacturer

▶ Supplier

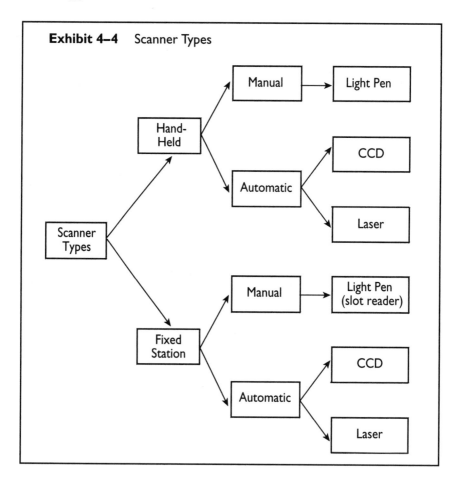

Exhibit 4–4 Scanner Types

- Light pen (wand scanner)
  —Makes contact with the label or surface on which pattern is printed
  —Inexpensive
  —Durable
  —Can be tied into various decoder types of equipment

- Charge Coupled Device (CCD)
  —Has a depth of field of several inches so you do not have to make contact with the label or other surface. Therefore, you can read through shrink wrap, which is common in warehousing operations.
  —Floods symbol with light and reflectance illuminates photodetectors in the CCD scanner. Can read very high bar code densities
  —Moderate cost

- Lasers
  —Project a beam of energy off of a rotating prism or oscillating mirror
  —Depth of field of several feet
  —Expensive but versatile

▶ SKU number
▶ Description
▶ Pack size
▶ Ship to address
▶ Bill to address
▶ Credit terms

Exhibit 4–5 Common Bar Code Print Technologies

- **Direct Thermal**—Overlapping dots are formed on a heat-sensitive substrate (label or other foundation) by selectively heating elements in a printhead.

- **Thermal Transfer**—Same concept as direct thermal except the image is transferred to the substrate from a ribbon that is heated by the elements in the printhead.

- **Dot Matrix Impact**—A moving printhead with rows of hammers that creates images through multiple passes over a ribbon.

- **Ink Jet**—A fixed printhead sprays tiny droplets of ink onto a substrate.

- **Laser (Xerographic)**—A controlled laser beam creates an image on an electrostatically charged, photoconductive drum. The charged areas attract toner particles that are transferred and fused onto the substrate.

▶ Identification of receiving clerk, stock replenishment worker, order filler, shipping clerk
▶ Shipper
▶ Carrier
▶ Quantity
▶ Throughput rates (e.g., pieces per hour)
▶ Time, date
▶ Location
▶ Purchase order identification

Think of all the information you need to control material in a manufacturing environment. For example:

▶ Particular bill of materials

▶ SKU number

▶ Quantity

▶ Work in process (WIP)

▶ Individual tasks

▶ Throughput rates

▶ Scrap

▶ Time, date

▶ Which machine

▶ Which process

▶ Location

▶ Machine instructions

▶ Job number

All of the above can be given a bar code identifier.

Bar code labels and markings can be printed directly on forms, boxes, the product itself, or on labels that are then affixed to forms, boxes, items themselves, individual parts of items, and so on.

A quick and easy way to begin using bar codes is through the use of scan boards or menu cards. A scan board or menu card is merely a sheet of paper or heavier card stock that contains on it information in both machine readable (bar code) and human readable (plain alpha-numeric text) formats. See Exhibit 4–6 for examples of common scan boards/menu cards.

Examples of using bar codes include:

▶ Receiving—Shipping

  1. Employee scans in their own identity off of scan board or identification badge.

Exhibit 4–6 Common Types of Bar Code Scan Boards/
Menu Cards

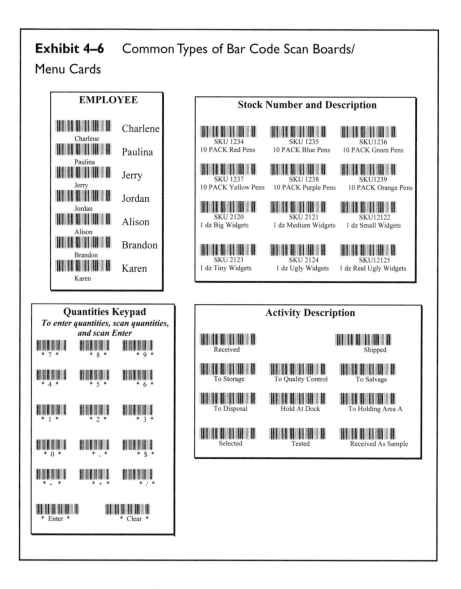

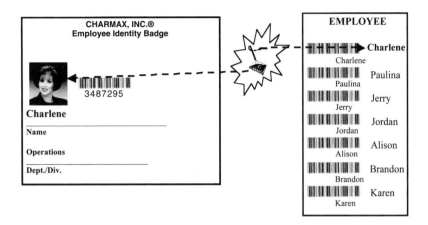

2. Employee scans product code from either items themselves or from scan board.

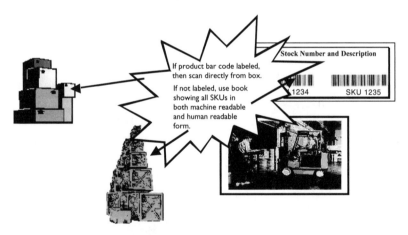

3. Employee scans in quantity.

4. Employee scans in activity (received, shipped, etc.).

▶ Tracking Multiple Activities at the Same Time in a Manufacturing Setting

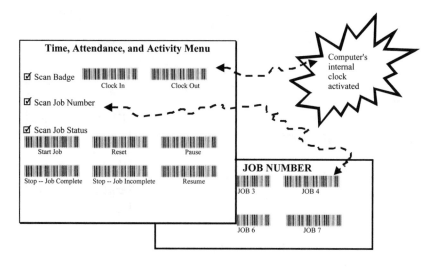

1. Employee scans in his or her identity.

2. Employee scans in either "Clock In" or "Clock Out." This starting/stopping time can be noted by the computer's internal clock. In addition, the computer's internal calendar notes the date.

   (a) This information could be automatically routed to accounting for payroll purposes.

   (b) This information will be captured for the particular job in question. That information can then be used as a part of various variance reports such as projected starting time versus actual starting time, projected ending time versus actual ending time, and so on. See Chapter 6, page 00–00 for a discussion of variance reports.

3. Employee scans in Job Number.

4. Employee scans in Job Status.

5. When employee scans in "Stop—Job Complete," system could begin, for example, a backflush of all raw materials used as part of the job just completed. See Exhibit 6–1

for more information on backflushing.

▶ Using Bar Coding as Part of a Maintenance Program

1. Bar codes are assigned to each part of the maintenance procedure and to various parts (engines, for example) of the piece of equipment in question.

2. Employee then uses a Time, Attendance, and Activity Menu to track the maintenance tasks.

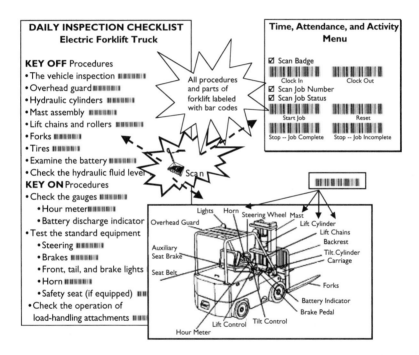

▶ Bar Coding and Physical Inventory and Cycle Counting

The Basics of Radio-Frequency Identification

Radio-frequency identification (RFID) is a generic term for technologies that use radio waves to automatically identify objects (or people). It is a still emerging overall set of technologies with no, as yet, universally accepted set of standards for label or tag layout, software or hardware design.

Although several methods of identification are available, the most common is to store a serial number that identifies an object and other information on a microchip. The microchip is attached to an antenna (the chip and the antenna together are called an RFID transponder, or an RFID tag). The antenna enables the chip to transmit the identification information to a reader. The reader converts the radio waves reflected back or sent from the RFID tag into digital information that can then be passed on to computers that can make use of it. See Exhibit 4–7.

Exhibit 4–7 RFID Components

▶ Bar coding is seeing; RFID is hearing.

RFID TAG TYPES AND CLASSES

There are two basic types and five basic classes of RFID tags.

The basic types are:

▶ *Passive Tags* — operate without an internal battery source. Electromagnetic waves sent from the reader starts a current in the tag's antenna, and the tag uses that energy to respond to the reader.

▶ *Active Tags* — powered by an internal battery and are typically read/write devices.

The tag classes include:

▶ *CLASS 0 (Read-Only Tags)* — Very basic tag with a minimum of data. Data is usually a simple Tag ID stored only once into the tag during manufacture.

---

1. Bar code markings in both machine-readable and human-readable form are placed on both the storage locations (shelves, racks, drawers, bins) and on the product itself.

2. A counter equipped with a portable scanner:

   a. Scans in the identity of the SKU.

   b. Enters the quantity through a keypad on the scanner. The record count and shelf count can be compared in a variety of ways:

   (1) The shelf count as captured by the scanner and counter can be transmitted into the system by way of radio frequency at the time of information capture, or it can be uploaded from the scanner at a later time. The computer system would then generate an exception report of those items where the record and shelf counts did not match.

   (2) Scanners are small computers. Because of that they can contain software allowing them to have the record count stored within them. As the scanner reads the bar code and the counter enters the quantity information, the scanner could immediately compare the record count and shelf count. If there was a discrepancy, the scanner could alert the counter either through audible tones, flashing lights, or LED displays. The counter could then immediately initiate a recount.

▶ *CLASS 1 (Write Once Read Only [WORM])* — These types of tags can be programmed by either the tag manufacturer or by the user only once.

▶ *CLASS 2 (Read Write)* — With these tags data can be read as well as written into the tag's memory.

▶ *CLASS 3 (Read Write with on-board sensors)* — These are active tags that contain sensors for recording parameters like temperature, pressure, etc., and can record the readings in tag memory.

▶ *CLASS 4 (Read Write with integrated transmitters)* — This class of tag can communicate with each other without any help from a reader.

The type of tag you use is dependent on how and why you're using RFID and the environment you're going to be operating it in. See Exhibit 4–8.

Bar Code versus RFID

Neither of these two technologies is necessarily better or worse than the other. They have different applications, which sometimes overlap. You must look at your application and your financial and technological resources when deciding which technology will work best for you — and, which you can afford both short and long term.

Only your imagination limits what you can use RFID for. Common uses include, but aren't limited to:

▶ *Asset tracking* — tracking of assets in offices, labs, warehouses, pallets and containers in the supply chain, books in libraries

▶ *Manufacturing* — tracking of parts during manufacture, tracking of assembled items

---

Exhibit 4–8 Tag Selection Considerations

- Data requirements — memory requirements, programmability, etc., will be dependent on use (e.g., item, box, case, pallet, returns).

- Type of reader — readers available to support the tag in question.

- Read speed — read speed will impact how long the tag has to be within range of the reader.

- Read redundancy — the number of times a tag must be read while in the reading area.

- Harsh environments — survivability and durability become factors in environments with high moisture (steam), corrosive chemicals, and high heat or extreme cold.

- Recordation — use may require tags to contain sensors that measure and record temperature, etc.

- Security — use may require tags to be capable of encryption.

▶ *Medical* — Linking patients to their specific drugs, personnel giving the drugs, biometric measurements

▶ *People tracking* — security tracking for entrance management or security, baby tags in hospitals to manage access to postnatal wards

▶ *Retail* — tracking grocery carts in supermarkets

▶ *Animal tracking* — implanted RFID tags in animals for tracking and linking the animal to food, location

▶ *Time tracking* — sports event timing to track athletes as they start a race and pass the finish line, pickup and delivery start and stop times

RFID Item Identification

One of the characteristics of RFID is that specific items in the supply chain can be individually identified. This is accomplished through a unique serial number. The dominant RFID code is the *Electronic Product Code™ (EPC)*. The unique serial number allows inquiries to be made about an item wherever it is within the supply chain. The most prevailing version of the EPC contains information about the manufacturer, the type of object, and a specific serial number that relates to the specific object being monitored.

The EPC and all protocols and standards relating to it are overseen by EPCglobal, a not-for-profit joint venture set up by the Uniform Code Council, which licensed the EPC technologies developed by the Auto-ID Center, and EAN International, the bar code standards body in Europe.

The Advantages of RFID

There are a number of advantages to RFID. See Exhibit 4–9.

Basically, bar codes are line-of-sight technology. A scanner has to "see" the bar code to read it. With RFID, tags can be read as long as they are within range of a reader. Bar codes can't see through objects or other barriers between the scanner and the reader. Radio waves, however, do travel through most barriers and are therefore far more versatile. (*Caution*: Radio waves bounce off metal and are absorbed by water at ultrahigh frequencies. Therefore, it's harder to RFID track metal objects or those with high water content. RFID designers and manufacturers continue to work on overcoming these issues.)

Exhibit 4–9 RFID Advantages

BAR CODES	RFID
• Require a direct line of sight to the printed barcode	Do not require a direct line of sight to the printed barcode. Can be read through most objects.
• Reading range generally up to 15 feet (depending on equipment)	Reading range up to approximately 300 feet (depending on equipment)
• Approximately a half second or more to successfully complete a read	Read rates up to 40 or more tags per second
• Bar code labels are more vulnerable. If a label is dirty, torn, falls off, etc., it can't be read.	RFID tags are more rugged because they are in a plastic cover and can even be embedded in a product (further protecting it from external forces)
• Barcodes have no read/write capability. Once printed no new information can be added.	RFID tags can be read/write devices. A RFID reader can communicate with the tag and alter as much of the information as the tag design will allow.
• Standard bar codes identify only the manufacturer and product, not the unique item (e.g., each widget is identified the same as every other identical widget — not that specific widget).	RFID tags identify the specific object.

The Problems Associated with RFID

Although RFID providers continue to improve RFID delivery mechanisms, configurations, and hardware and software, there are a number of challenges associated with RFI.

LACK OF RFID STANDARDS

Because global standards are still being developed, different manufacturers have implemented RFID in a variety of ways, Many of these installations are "closed-loop" systems. In a nutshell, this means that a company has implemented a system to track items that never leave its own control using a certain proprietary technology. Therefore, a different organization that has implanted RFID using a different RFID technology can't read the tags that were placed by the first company, and vice versa.

Many of the supply chain benefits of RFID are derived from being able to track items as they move from one organization to the next or, even, internationally. The lack of standardization frustrates those benefits.

MONEY, MONEY, MONEY

Cost continues to be a major consideration.

RFID readers typically cost hundreds of dollars. You must calculate how many readers you would need to cover all of your locations. Some companies would need hundreds, if not thousands, of readers to cover all their factories, warehouses, and stores.

RFID tags can also become expensive to the point of being cost prohibitive. Even if a tag only cost 10 to 20 cents, imagine the expense of placing hundreds of thousands of them on an item that only costs a few dollars.

SYSTEM DISRUPTION VULNERABILITY

Because RFID systems use the electromagnetic spectrum, they are relatively easy to jam using energy at the right frequency.

In addition, active RFID tags that use a battery to increase the range of the system can be repeatedly interrogated to wear the battery down, resulting in system disruption.

RFID READER COLLISION

When the signals from two or more readers overlap, reader collision occurs. The tag is unable to respond to simultaneous queries.

Many systems use an *anticollision protocol* (also called a *singulation protocol*) that enable tags to take turns in transmitting to a reader.

RFID TAG COLLISION

Tag collision occurs when many tags are present in a small area and are trying to send information simultaneously to the reader.

RFID providers are developing systems that ensure that tags respond one at a time.

SECURITY, PRIVACY, AND ETHICS PROBLEMS WITH RFID

▶ The contents of an RFID tag can be read in a pocket or purse. Since RFID tags cannot tell the difference between one reader and another and scanners are portable, RFID tags in your pocket or purse can be read from a distance, from a few inches to a few yards.

▶ RFID tags are difficult to remove. RFID tags are difficult to for consumers to remove, irritating them.

▶ RFID tags with unique serial numbers could be linked to an individual credit card number

The Universal Product Code (UPC) implemented with bar codes only allows each product type sold in a store to have a unique number that identifies that product. However, all of that product would have the same number — not a unique number for each individual item. In an RFID system *each individual item* can have its own number. With that type of a system in place, if an item is scanned for purchase and is paid for, the RFID tag number for a particular item could be associated with a credit card number.

Recap

The objective of this chapter was to provide you with an overview of automated identification approaches including bar coding, various popular symbologies, basic bar code applications, and radio-frequency identification.

The set of rules for how the bars and spaces of a bar code language, its symbology, are arranged dictates how much and what type of data can be displayed within a particular symbol. The language that is most appropriate to your industry will be determined by how much data and in what form that information must be displayed on your goods, inventory, or other materials.

RFID is a technology that has a wide array of potential uses. Although there are real challenges in implementing an RFID system, with proper implementation, RFID is a technology that can improve your supply chain process—and your bottom line.

In applying automated identification to your system, you are only limited by your imagination—and your wallet. Applications can be simple ones involving bar code scan boards or can be complex, utilizing laser scanners, radio frequency, and sophisticated sharing of information throughout the system at the time of information capture.

REVIEW QUESTIONS

1. True or False

   The Universal Product Code allows for the identification of each individual item sold in a retail environment.

   (a) True
   (b) False

2. True or False

   There are only five types of bar code languages.

   (a) True

   (b) False

3. True or False

   The most widely used bar code symbology for nonretail applications is Code 39.

   (a) True

   (b) False

4. True or False

   When the signals from two or more readers overlap, tag collision occurs.

   (a) True

   (b) False

5. Which symbology is the most widely used for retail point-of-sale transactions?

   (a) Universal Product Code

   (b) Code 39

   (c) Code 128

   (d) Codabar

Answers

1. (b), 2. (b), 3. (a), 4. (b), 5. (a)

CHAPTER 5

PLANNING AND REPLENISHMENT CONCEPTS

The objective of this chapter is to provide basic approaches to forecasting inventory levels and to undertaking stock replenishment. With the proper techniques, you will have the right item, in the right quantity, at the right time, and in the right place.

Replenishment Costs

As discussed in Chapter 2, every day that an item remains in your stockroom costs you money in the form of a carrying cost (K Factor). If you take that concept to its extreme, it would make sense to only buy items exactly when you need them. Multiple smaller quantity purchases of the same item certainly hold down your carrying costs. However, it hurts your cost of replenishment—the expenses associated with buying things.

It costs money to buy things. That sounds absurdly simple when you first read it. However, the cost of purchasing product exceeds the actual price paid for it. Expenses related to purchasing include the salaries of the purchasing staff, rent, and other overhead expenses attributable to the purchasing department. See Exhibit 5–1.

In fact, the more often you buy, the greater your internal costs. For example, if you purchased one million widgets all at the same time, your purchasing or replenishment cost (R Factor) would be

---

Exhibit 5–1 Calculating the R Factor

The cost of replenishment is calculated on a per item, per order basis. This is because it takes the same amount of internal effort to determine how much of each item you desire, from which supplier, at what pricing, terms, and so on, no matter which item is being considered and no matter how many items there are on any given PO. Therefore, if the R Factor is $5.00 per item, per order, and there is a single line item on an order, the replenishment cost is $5.00. If there are two items, it's $10.00. If there are three items, it's $15.00, and so on.[1]

To calculate the cost of replenishment, include:

Annual cost of purchasing department labor	$220,000
Annual cost of purchasing department overhead (rent, utilities, equipment allocation, etc.)	$179,000
Annual cost of expediting stock items	$25,000
Total annual costs	$424,000
Number of purchase orders created per year for stock (assume):	10,000
Average number of different stock items per order (assume):	× 8
Total number of times stock items were ordered:	80,000

$$\frac{\text{Total Annual Costs}}{\text{Total Times Stock Items Were Ordered}} = \longrightarrow \frac{\text{R Factor}}{} = \frac{\$424,000}{80,000} = \boxed{\$5.30 = \text{R Factor}}$$

the cost per line item per purchase order (PO). See Exhibit 5–1.

▸ If the per line, per PO cost is $5.00, then your cost to buy all one million widgets at one time would be $5.00.

▸ If you were to buy the same one million widgets 250,000 at a time, then your R Factor would be $5.00 times four (four POs with one line item each) or $20.00.

▸ If you purchased the widgets one at a time, the cost would be one million times $5.00 or $5 million.

Order size versus frequency of purchase shifts the cost burden from the K Factor to the R Factor and vice versa. In other words:

▸ If you buy smaller quantities more often, your purchasing costs go up, which means your R Factor increases.

▸ If you buy larger quantities less often, you have a higher inventory level for a longer period of time, so your carrying costs go up, which means your K Factor increases.

▸ In a perfect world the K Factor and the R Factor would be equal. Although this is difficult to achieve, an organization attempting to have the correct amount of product at the overall lowest cost will strive for that balance.

Types of Inventory Management

In the worlds of distribution, retailing, and replacement parts, an organization deals with finished goods. In the manufacturing world, an organization deals with raw materials and subassemblies. Considerations of what to buy, when to buy it, in what quantities, and so on are dramatically different in these two worlds.

In distribution, you are concerned with having the right item in the right quantity. Issues relating to having the item at the right time and place are often dealt with by simply increasing safety

Case Study: Balancing Carrying and Replenishment Costs

A dispute has arisen at the Charmax Co. between the purchasing and warehouse managers.

Charmax's receiving ends at 5:00 PM. At 4:45 PM, a 40-foot trailer is backed up to the dock. The doors are opened to reveal three levels of floor-stacked boxes extending from floor to ceiling, back to front.

Joe, the warehouse manager, realizes that it will take four workers at least two hours to hand unload the trailer. Virtually all of that time will be on an overtime basis.

Joe reviews the truck's manifest and determines what items on the trailer are needed for delivery tomorrow morning. He discovers that there are only three boxes on the trailer that are truly required for tomorrow's business. He asks Tracy, the truck driver, if he helped to load the trailer. Tracy replies that he did. Joe asks if Tracy remembers where those three boxes are. With a smile, Tracy replies that they are located in the nose of the trailer.

Joe decides not to incur the overtime. He will have the trailer unloaded in the morning.

Betty, the sales manager, hears that the three items will not be shipped to Acme, a large and important customer. She storms into the warehouse and demands that the trailer be unloaded.

Joe explains the overtime situation. Betty replies that Joe should have scheduled the trailer to arrive earlier in the day. Joe replies that the buyer, Bill, handles traffic management as part of the purchase of the product. Betty angrily says she doesn't much care. Joe had told her that the product would be here today for delivery tomorrow. "You promised me," Betty says, "so that's what I promised the customer. Now unload the trailer." Joe reluctantly does so.

Later, Joe confronts Bill and demands that product be brought in palletized or unitized or in some other manner so it can be unloaded quickly. Joe argues that since internal handling is a major component in computing the cost of carrying inventory, unitization will help cut Charmax's costs.

Bill responds that he has to buy the product as he is buying it now. He argues that to palletize the product would increase the costs per unit of product. He also points out that since the product already extends to the top of the trailer, that the added height of three levels of pallets at approximately four inches each, would force him to buy less per order so that it will all fit on a trailer. Therefore, he will have to buy less and buy it more often, driving up his replenishment costs. Ill-will and stalemate result.

Suggested Solutions:

1. Joe and Bill should coordinate traffic management so that loads match the labor, equipment, time resources, and constraints of the organization. By lowering handling costs the company will reduce overall carrying costs.

2. Both Joe and Bill need to specifically determine their respective costs.
   (a) Joe can determine the handling portion of the K Factor by:
      (1) Determining the average time it takes to hand unload a trailer.
      (2) Multiplying the average hand unloading time times the number of trailers during the year.
      (3) Multiplying the total hand unloading time times the average hourly labor rate being paid the warehouse personnel.

(continues)

(continued.)

(4) Determining the average time it would take to unload unitized loads.

(5) Multiplying the average unitized unloading time times the number of trailers during the year.

(6) Multiplying the total unitized unloading time times the average hourly labor rate being paid the warehouse personnel.

(7) Comparing the annual labor costs involved for hand unloading to the annual labor costs of unitized unloading to determine the total dollar savings.

(b) Bill can determine his added replenishment costs associated with smaller loads purchased more often.

(c) A fair comparison can then be made as to which route is the most advantageous for the overall organization.

3. Alternatives meeting the needs of both parties might be developed. For example, if slip-sheets (thin cardboard or plywood sheets the same length and width as a pallet) were used, Bill might be able to overcome the size of load and volume problem, while Joe could automate the unloading process.

stock on hand. That is not a good solution because it leads to wasted money and space. However, traditional formulae used to compute inventory requirements in a distribution environment focus on item and quantity rather than place and time. In manufacturing, you are concerned with having the right item, in the right quantity, at the right time, in the right place.

Demand for finished goods and spare parts for replacements

are said to be "independent," while demand for items in the manufacturing world are said to be "dependent." Understanding these distinctions will assist you in forecasting your procurement needs.

Independent demand is influenced by market conditions outside the control of your organization's operations. The demand for the widgets your organization sells will be independent of the demand for your gadgets, doodads, and whatchamacallits. Your products are independent of one another. In this environment, you must have the right item in the right quantity.

Dependent demand is related to another item. The demand for products built up or created from raw materials, parts, and assemblies is dependent on the demand for the final product. You would not need one item if you did not also require another, both of which would go into an assembly or finished product. In this environment, you must have the right items in the right quantities at the time to complete a finished product.

A chair can be used as an example. The demand for the number of chairs you need is independent from the number of tables that you need because quantity required is influenced by the demand in the market for each item. The demand for chair legs or seats or rails is mathematically dependent on the demand for finished chairs. Four legs and one seat are required for each chair.

Dependent and independent demands demonstrate very different use and demand patterns.

Independent demand calls for a replenishment approach to inventory management. This approach assumes that market forces will exhibit a somewhat fixed pattern. Therefore, stock is replenished as it is used in order to have items on hand for customers.

Dependent demand calls for a requirements approach. When an assembly or finished item is needed, then the materials needed to create it are ordered. There is no fixed pattern because an assembly created in the past may never be produced again.

The nature of demand, therefore, leads to different concepts, formulae, and methods of inventory management.

INDEPENDENT DEMAND INVENTORY

Since items in an independent demand inventory system "stand alone," the appropriate reorder point for each item must be calculated using *order-point formulae.*

Order-Point Formulae

Order-point formulae are used to determine how much of a given item needs to be ordered where there is independent demand. In these formulae, a reorder point (ROP) is set for each item. The ROP is the lowest amount of an item you will have on hand and on order before you reorder.

A Simple Min-Max Inventory System

Order-point formulae are based on some relatively simple concepts.

Imagine that all of a particular SKU are kept in a single bin. If no reorder point was set, then the entire batch would be used up without any order being placed. The organization would then be unable to sell or use that item during whatever timeframe—was required to order and bring the SKU in the lead time. It would therefore make sense to adopt a two-bin system, with Bin 1 containing working stock and Bin 2 containing working reserve. The amount of product in Bin 2 would be equal to your usage rate during that item's lead time.

In a two-bin system, if all goes as it should, then immediately on using the first item from Bin 2, you would reorder a quantity equal to both Bins 1 and 2. As you use the last item in Bin 2, the order arrives and you refill both bins. This assumes that lead time is exact, there are no vendor stockouts or backorders, and that there are never any defects. That assumption is, of course, often false. Therefore, a true order-point system is a three-bin system, with Bin 3 containing safety stock.

Bin 3, safety stock, relates to Bin 2 since Bin 3 is to make up for uncertainties in lead time and defects. Mathematically safety stock is 50 percent of working reserve. (The average between having nothing in Bin 2 and having it at 100 percent full is 50 percent.) However, companies adjust safety stock levels to coincide with their actual experience.

Bins can be mathematically created or can reflect actual physical separation of items in the stockroom.

A simple formula for determining the ROP reflects the above concepts.

$$(\text{Usage} \times \text{Lead Time}) + \text{Safety Stock} = \text{ROP}$$

In the above formula lead time is shown as a percentage of a month, as follows:

1 week	= 0.25	= 25%	4 weeks	= 1.00	= 100%
2 weeks	= 0.50	= 50%	5 weeks	= 1.25	= 125%
3 weeks	= 0.75	= 75%	6 weeks	= 1.50	= 150%

Example 1
Assumptions:

- Usage rate of 1,200 items per month
- Lead time of 3 weeks

Step-by-Step Calculation:

- Calculate weekly usage. Assume a 4-week month. 1,200 items ÷ 4 weeks = 300 items per week, therefore Bin 1 or working stock should contain at least 300 items

- Calculate working reserve: Given 3 weeks of lead time, working reserve should be 1,200 items × 0.75 = 900 items
- Calculate safety stock, use 50 percent of working reserve as a guideline (900 items × 50% = 450 items)
- Calculate ROP: (1,200 items × 0.75) + 450 items = ROP 1,350 items

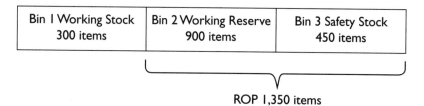

Example 2
Assumptions:

- Usage rate of 1,200 items per month
- Lead time of 1 week

Step-by-Step Calculation:

- Calculate weekly usage. Assume a 4-week month. 1,200 items ÷ 4 weeks = 300 items per week, therefore Bin 1 or working stock should contain at least 300 items
- Calculate working reserve: Given 1 week of lead time, working reserve should be 1,200 items × 0.25 = 300 items
- Calculate safety stock, use 50 percent of working reserve as a guideline (300 items × 50% = 150 items)
- Calculate ROP: (1,200 items× 0.25) + 150 items = ROP 450 items

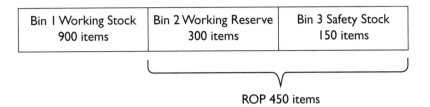

| Bin 1 Working Stock
900 items | Bin 2 Working Reserve
300 items | Bin 3 Safety Stock
150 items |

ROP 450 items

The ROP is the "minimum" (min) in a "minimum-maximum" (min-max) inventory control system. In these systems there is a minimum below which you will not let your stock level fall, and there is a maximum above which you will not have items on hand or on order.

To compute the maximum in these systems, you must first determine how often you will place orders. This time period is called the review cycle.

The review cycle is the length of time between reviews of when you wish to order product. The formula to determine the review cycle is:

$$\frac{\text{Total Purchases from Vendor for a Year}}{\text{Discount Quantity}} = \text{Review Cycle}$$

The unit of measure reflecting total purchases from a vendor can be dollars, pieces, pounds, units, or whatever your organization uses. The discount quantity is the minimum amount you have to order of that unit of measure in order to be granted a discount.

Review Cycle Example

$$\frac{200,000}{5,000} = \text{Review Cycle}$$

And, dividing 40 reviews by 52 weeks equals a review roughly every 1.3 weeks. When the review actually occurs will also depend on factors such as seasonality.

The maximum in these systems is also represented by a simple formula.

ROP + Usage During the Review Cycle = Maximum

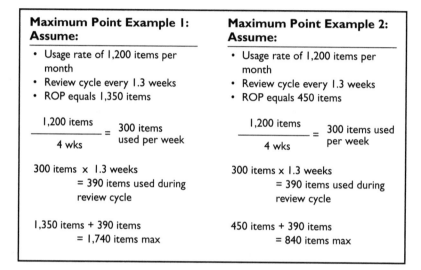

Maximum Point Example 1: **Assume:**	**Maximum Point Example 2:** **Assume:**
• Usage rate of 1,200 items per month	• Usage rate of 1,200 items per month
• Review cycle every 1.3 weeks	• Review cycle every 1.3 weeks
• ROP equals 1,350 items	• ROP equals 450 items
$\dfrac{1{,}200 \text{ items}}{4 \text{ wks}} = 300$ items used per week	$\dfrac{1{,}200 \text{ items}}{4 \text{ wks}} = 300$ items used per week
300 items x 1.3 weeks = 390 items used during review cycle	300 items x 1.3 weeks = 390 items used during review cycle
1,350 items + 390 items = 1,740 items max	450 items + 390 items = 840 items max

By setting a min-max for each item in your inventory, you can create a simple method of ordering products having independent demand.

ECONOMIC ORDER QUANTITY FORMULA

In 1915, F. W. Harris of General Electric developed the Economic Order Quantity (EOQ) formula to help stockkeepers in determining how much product to buy.

To calculate EOQ, assume:

$$A = \text{Total Value of SKU Per Year}$$
$$K = \text{Carrying Cost (the K Factor)}$$
$$R = \text{Replenishment Cost (the R Factor)}$$

P = Price Per Unit

Basic Formula

$$EOQ = \sqrt{\frac{2AR}{P^2K}}$$

This formula and its variations allow you to determine the following:

▶ Optimal quantity to order
▶ When it should be ordered
▶ Total cost
▶ Average inventory level
▶ How much should be ordered each time
▶ Maximum inventory level

The EOQ model is based on several assumptions:

▶ The demand rate is constant (no variations), recurring, and known.
▶ The carrying cost and ordering cost are independent of the quantity ordered (no discounts).
▶ The lead time is constant and known. Therefore, the ordering times given result in new orders arriving exactly when the inventory level reaches zero.
▶ The formula can handle only one type of item at a time.
▶ Orders arrive in a single batch (no vendor stockouts or backorders).

A simple example of the basic formula is:

A = $36,000
K = 15%

$$R = \$75$$
$$P = \$25$$

$$EOQ = \sqrt{\frac{2AR}{P^2K}} = \sqrt{\frac{2(\$36,000)(\$75)}{(\$25)^2(0.15)}} = \sqrt{\frac{5,475,000}{93.75}} = \sqrt{58,400}$$
$$= 242 \text{ units per order}$$

Since the above assumptions do not reflect the real world, mathematicians have developed variations of the basic formula. See Exhibit 5–2.

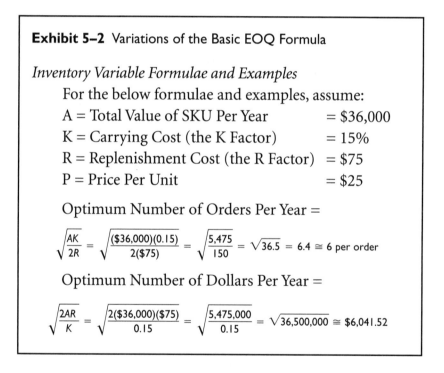

Exhibit 5–2 Variations of the Basic EOQ Formula

Inventory Variable Formulae and Examples

For the below formulae and examples, assume:

A = Total Value of SKU Per Year = \$36,000
K = Carrying Cost (the K Factor) = 15%
R = Replenishment Cost (the R Factor) = \$75
P = Price Per Unit = \$25

Optimum Number of Orders Per Year =

$$\sqrt{\frac{AK}{2R}} = \sqrt{\frac{(\$36,000)(0.15)}{2(\$75)}} = \sqrt{\frac{5,475}{150}} = \sqrt{36.5} = 6.4 \cong 6 \text{ per order}$$

Optimum Number of Dollars Per Year =

$$\sqrt{\frac{2AR}{K}} = \sqrt{\frac{2(\$36,000)(\$75)}{0.15}} = \sqrt{\frac{5,475,000}{0.15}} = \sqrt{36,500,000} \cong \$6,041.52$$

How to Set Up an EOQ Worksheet in Microsoft® Excel®

Here's a tip. By setting up a permanent worksheet in Microsoft® Excel® or similar spreadsheet program, you will be able to quickly calculate important EOQ information simply by entering variable values for A, K, R, and P under the "Insert Value" column.

Based on the cell placement as noted below, you can calculate each quantity by entering the following formulae:

Economic Order Quantity → type: = SQRT((2*E4*E8)/((E10 ^2)*E6))

Optimum Number of Orders Per Year → type: = SQRT((E4*E6)/(2*E8))

Optimum Number of Dollars Per Order → type: = SQRT((2*E4*E8)/E6)

DEPENDENT DEMAND INVENTORY

Materials Requirements Planning

Controlling not only what item is purchased and in what quantities, but also the timing of its arrival through computerized systems is called *materials requirements planning* (*MRP*). This concept of the right item, in the right quantity, and at the right time was first introduced by Joseph Orlicky in the early 1960s.

Independent demand inventory management is customer oriented. The objective of ROP rules and formulae is high customer service levels and low operating costs. Dependent demand systems, however, are manufacturing oriented. The objective of dependent demand inventory control is to support the master production schedule. Even if you have a low stock level of an item, it won't be ordered unless and until it is needed to produce something for the master schedule—a true requirements philosophy of inventory control. MRP-dependent demand inventory control is directed inward rather than outward like ROP inventory control. See Exhibit 5–3.

Exhibit 5–3 Contrasting Order Point with MRP Systems

	ORDER POINT	MRP
Demand	Independent	Dependent
Order Philosophy	Replenishment	Requirements
Forecasting	Based on past demand	Based on master schedule
Control Concept	ABC categorization	All items are equally important
Objectives	Meet customer needs	Meet manufacturing needs
Lot Sizing	EOQ	Individual item requirements
Demand Pattern	Consistent	Random but predictable
Inventory Type	Finished goods/ spare parts	Work in progress/ raw materials

MRP Elements. Key concepts in understanding MRP are the master production schedule and the bill of materials.

The master production schedule sets out what will be built, when, and in what quantities. It can either cover short or long time horizons.

Short horizon—planning of initial requirements sets out:

▶ Final product requirements

▶ Schedule for production of components

▶ Purchase order priorities

▶ Short-term capacity requirements

Long horizon—estimating long-term requirements sets out:

▶ Long-term production capacity required

▶ Long-term warehouse capacity required

▶ Long-term staffing required

▶ Long-term money required

The *bill of materials* (BOM) is the recipe of raw materials, parts, subassemblies, and so on required to build or make something.

Each BOM has levels. See Exhibit 5–4 and Exhibit 6–1 on page 175 for a discussion of how inventory is relieved from stock after each level of the BOM is completed. This is a technique called "backflushing."

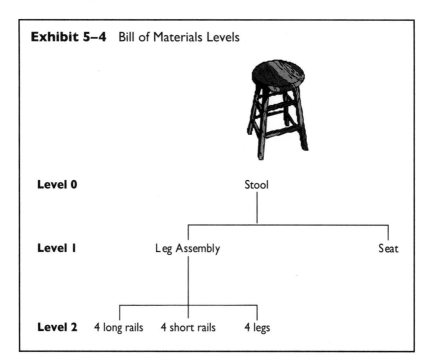

Exhibit 5–4 Bill of Materials Levels

Level 0 Stool

Level I Leg Assembly Seat

Level 2 4 long rails 4 short rails 4 legs

MRP's chief advantage over the ROP approach is that it lets you customize your ordering strategy for raw materials, parts, and so on with different demand characteristics, such as lead times. The ROP approach answers the questions of *what* and *how much*:

On Hand	60	or	60
On Order	100		50
Required	130		130
	———		———
Available	30		-20

ROP does not answer the question of *when*:

On Hand	60		or	60
On Order	100 due in on Nov. 15th			50 due on Nov. 1st
Required	130 needed by Nov. 5th			100 needed by Nov. 5th

30 needed by Nov. 15th

Available when needed		−70	10 on Nov. 5th −20 on Nov. 15th

MRP allows purchases to be made as and when needed to ensure that items will arrive when needed. It accomplishes this by setting up time phasing charts within the computer system. See Exhibit 5–5.

An example of MRP would be a decision to build one bar stool in your garage on Saturday.

The decision to build a single unit of something on a given day is the master schedule.

Included in your thinking was the fact that if you had all of the pieces, parts, and tools necessary, you could actually accomplish the task. That is rough-cut capacity planning. See Exhibit 5–6.

You then draw-up and define what parts are required for the task. See Exhibit 5–4. This is your bill of materials.

Exhibit 5–5 Time Phasing Chart for a Single Item Within a MRP System

Assumptions:

- 12-week production schedule
- 10 units of this item are required each week for production
- Starting balance of 70 units
- One week lead time

As evidenced by the first chart, you do not need to buy and hold any of the items in question until Week 7. Week 7's production will bring our balance of inventory on hand to zero.

Time Phasing Chart Without Release of Purchase Order

0	1	2	3	4	5	6	7	8	9	10	11	12	Week Number
	10	10	10	10	10	10	10	10	10	10	10	10	Gross Requirements
													Scheduled Receipt
70	60	50	40	30	20	10	0	–10	–20	–30	–40	–50	Inventory on Hand
													Planned Order Release

Time Phasing Chart With Release of Purchase Order

0	1	2	3	4	5	6	7	8	9	10	11	12	Week Number
	10	10	10	10	10	10	10	10	10	10	10	10	Gross Requirements
						100							Scheduled Receipt
70	60	50	40	30	20	10	100	90	80	70	60	50	Inventory on Hand
					100								Planned Order Release

In the second chart, a purchase order is released during Week 6. The product arrives during Week 7, and you are ready for production as Week 8 begins.

The above charts demonstrate that by timing the release of the PO for a specific item, that item can be brought in only when needed. This holds our inventory levels down.

The next step is a parts explosion, during which you review your on-hand inventory levels to initially determine if any POs must be prepared and released.

You then engage in detailed capacity planning to decide if you can proceed or if the master schedule, capacity, or the planned release of POs must be changed.

Ultimately, all parts, equipment, and so on come together and the stool is built.

MRP works well because it is a forward-looking system. The predictability of events allows for careful planning and a reduction

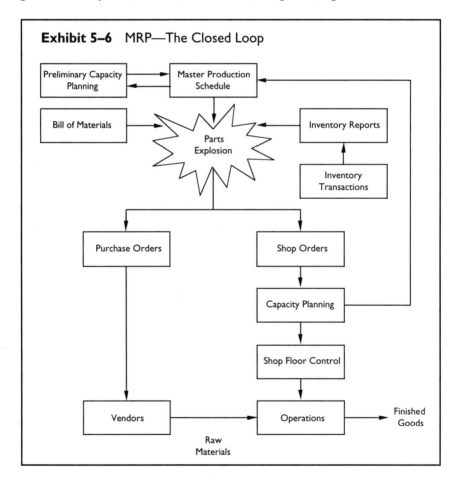

Exhibit 5–6 MRP—The Closed Loop

in unnecessary inventory.

A major drawback of MRP and JIT systems is that they are highly data dependent. Not only do you have to have all of the data easily available on an ongoing basis, but, in addition, the information must be accurate and timely. Organizations lacking a strong software/hardware infrastructure will have difficulty in fully implementing an MRP system.

Just-in-Time (JIT) Inventory Systems

JIT was first developed within Toyota's manufacturing operations by Taiichi Ohno in the 1970s as a means of meeting customer demands with minimum delay. In its original form, it referred to the production of goods, assemblies, and subassemblies to meet exactly the customer's demand in terms of time, quality, and quantity. With a JIT system, the "buyer" can be the actual end user or another process along the production line.

JIT goes further than MRP, because you control not only the right item, in the right quantity, at the right time, but you also bring that SKU to the right place. Under this time-based concept, an item appears exactly when it is needed—not before, not after.

The American Production and Inventory Control Society (APICS) has the following definition of JIT:

> . . . a philosophy of manufacturing based on planned elimination of all waste and continuous improvement of productivity. It encompasses the successful execution of all manufacturing activities required to produce a final product, from design engineering to delivery and including all stages of conversion from raw material onward. The primary elements include having only the required inventory when needed; to improve quality to zero defects; to reduce lead time by reducing setup times, queue lengths and lot sizes; to incrementally revise the operations themselves; and to accomplish these things at minimum cost.

The many benefits of a JIT system include:

▶ Reduction of stockouts

▶ Reduction of inventory levels

▶ Reduction of need for material handling equipment

▶ Reduction of timeframes between delivery and production

▶ Significant quality improvement

▶ Employee inclusion in continuous quality improvement

JIT is a management philosophy rather than a technique.

The fact that certain words and acronyms have come to be used somewhat interchangeably can be confusing to anyone not in the manufacturing world. Do those terms/acronyms have individual, stand-alone characteristics differentiating one from the other? Most certainly they do, but grappling with the details of what separates one particular type of manufacturing philosophy from another closely related theory won't further your understanding of the basic concepts of inventory management and control.

The terms/acronyms MRP III, Computer-Integrated Manufacturing, Lean Manufacturing, Short-Cycle Manufacturing, Just-in-Time, JIT, Enterprise Resource Planning, ERP, and so on all relate to the fundamental notions that:

▶ Manufacturing activities should be integrated.

▶ The actions and decisions of each department should complement all other departments.

▶ Information should flow both internally throughout the organization and externally to/from suppliers/customers electronically rather than through:

• The movement of hard paper copies, or

• Individual software (accounting) modules whose data

do not flow into one another both automatically and in real time.

▶ Suppliers are reliable and raw materials are without defect.

▶ All employees follow the philosophy of continuous quality improvement in all aspects of the operation.

Let's concentrate on how these concepts—by whatever name—relate to inventory. They all regard inventory as *waste*.

Today JIT has come to mean producing with a minimum of waste. "Waste" is used in the broadest sense and includes any non-value-adding activities. For example, storing, inspecting, and counting materials doesn't change the items; therefore, those actions add no value. There are seven types of waste JIT systems strive to eliminate:

1. Overproduction—producing more than needed. Wasted money, effort, space, etc.

2. Waiting time—decreases productivity and efficiency.

3. Transportation-double and even triple handling of an item from one storage position to another.

4. Processing—what are the interfaces between parties, departments, you, and your suppliers? The fewer and faster the better.

5. Inventory—stock simply sitting around does no one any good.

6. Motion—reduce motions such as those involved in looking for materials.

7. Defects—defective goods not only cost money directly, but they also cause stops and delays.

Implementing JIT. Take the following steps to introduce a JIT-type system into your manufacturing facility:

1. *Stabilize and level the production schedule.*

   - All work centers should have a uniform load through constant daily production.

   - Prevent changes in the production plan for some period of time.

   - Produce roughly the same mix of products each day, using a repeating sequence if several products are produced on the same line. This is often called "mixed model assembly."

   - Change the quantity of end-item inventory to meet demand fluctuations rather than through fluctuations in production levels.

2. *Reduce or eliminate setup times.*

   - Strive to create single-digit setup times (less than 10 minutes).

3. *Reduce lot sizes (manufacturing and purchase).*

   - Reducing setup times allows economical production of smaller lots.

   - Close cooperation with suppliers is necessary to achieve reductions in order lot sizes since more frequent deliveries will be called for. In JIT systems, the old, adversarial methods of purchasing will not work. In traditional approaches, buyers buy an item here and another item there through a series of disconnected negotiations over price, delivery quality, and terms. In JIT systems, larger quantities and types of items are purchased from fewer vendors. The larger purchases give the buyer more economic leverage while providing the supplier with enough financial incentive to become the buyer's business partner. Both parties recognize the critical needs, costing, pricing, quality concerns, and so on of the other.

4. *Reduce lead times (production and delivery).*
   - Production lead times can be reduced by:
     - Moving workstations closer together.
     - Applying group technology and cellular manufacturing concepts.
     - Reducing the number of jobs waiting to be processed at a given machine ("queue" length).
     - Improving the coordination and cooperation between successive processes, such as reducing delivery times by inducing suppliers to have distribution centers/warehouses closer to your operation.

5. *Engage in strong preventive maintenance.*
   - Machine and worker idle time should be used to maintain equipment and prevent breakdowns.

6. *Cross-train to create a flexible workforce.*
   - Workers should be trained to:
     - Operate several machines.
     - Perform maintenance tasks.
     - Perform quality inspections.

7. *Require supplier quality assurance and implement a zero-defects quality program.*
   - Since there are no buffers of safety stock, errors leading to defective items must be eliminated.

8. *Use a control system such as a kanban (card) system to convey parts between workstations in small quantities (ideally, one unit at a time).*

INVENTORY OBJECTIVES

Inventory in and of itself is not waste. *Unnecessary* inventory is waste. A key question is: What is unnecessary in the context of your organization?

In manufacturing operations, inventory in excess of that needed to support current operations or research and development efforts would certainly be waste. However, is the inventory of a distributor that uses immediate availability of a large cross-section of items as an effective, profitable marketing tool "unnecessary?"

Your company should have a "zero-tolerance" inventory policy. That is, it will not accept any inventory over a stated target. But what is the target? Is it zero-tolerance from a days' supply of inventory on hand? Is it a zero-tolerance from a dollars-invested standpoint (turns per year)? Is it zero-tolerance from an order fill rate of 97 percent?

For an organization to actually have useful inventory, it must understand its own objectives for the product it will have on hand, on-order, or in-transit at any one time. What inventory level is required for your organization to profitably and effectively operate?

Until the answers to these questions are determined, it will be difficult to get everyone within the organization to work toward the common, shared goal of eliminating inventory waste.

Enterprise Resource Planning

A significant way for any organization to pull together all of the diverse elements of information it needs to more effectively acquire and control inventory is to use enterprise resource planning. *Enterprise resource planning* (ERP) is an integrated computer-based information system that is used to manage both internal and external resources serving all departments within an enterprise, as shown in Exhibit 5–7.

Because different departments within a company have different functions and needs—for instance, the particular interests and needs of a company's finance department are certainly different than those of its human resources, production planning and operations, warehousing, sales, and other departments—it's typical for each department to have software systems, information flows, and operations optimized for the ways that department works.

In addition, because information generally moves through the system at different speeds than the physical movement of inventory, there are often significant disconnects in who knows what, when they know it, and what they do with it. (See Chapter 1 for a discussion of inventory as both a tangible and intangible item.)

ERP involves the use of packaged software rather than proprietary software written by or for one customer. With this software, which integrates all departments and functions of a company into a single, integrated computer system that runs off a single database, one department is able to "see" the information contained in another department. This allows all departments within a company to share information more easily and to communicate with each other more effectively.

Integrated ERP software is divided into software modules that roughly approximate the old stand-alone systems, such as manufacturing, order entry, accounts receivable and payable, general ledger, purchasing, warehousing, transportation, and human resources. Departments get the equivalent of their former stand-alone system, however, now the modules are linked so that someone in accounting can see if an order has been shipped, and the sales department can determine when an item will be available for sale or use.

Most ERP vendors' systems are flexible enough to allow, with varying degrees of effort, modules to interface with an organization's own software and, depending on the software, ERP modules may be alterable by the enterprise itself. Many companies only install one or two ERP modules at a time rather than trying to install

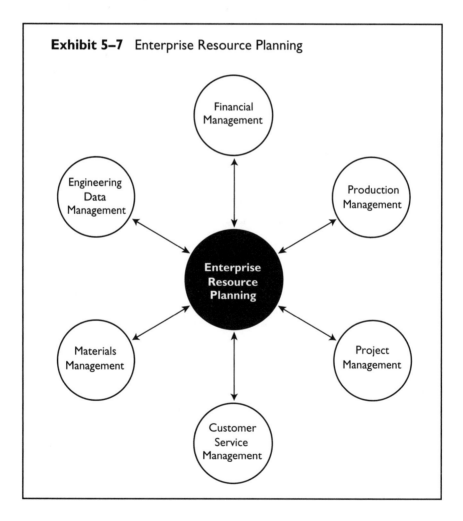

Exhibit 5–7 Enterprise Resource Planning

everything at once.

The benefits of installing ERP can be tremendous. Imagine the efficiencies gained if a salesperson can immediately know the credit limits of a customer from the finance module as well as if the warehouse has in stock the items that customer wants from the warehouse module, and so on.

The five main reasons organizations implement ERP are:

1. Integration of financial information—all business units use the same set of metrics.

2. Integration of customer order information—customer information is available to all business units on a real-time basis.

3. Standardization of manufacturing processes—standardization of processes leads to operating efficiencies.

4. Reduction of inventory—excess inventory is held to a minimum.

5. Standardization of human resources information—uniformity of information and access leads to better administration.

Actually implementing an ERP system can be expensive, time consuming, and difficult.

One of the greatest challenges to ERP implementation isn't so much the installation of the software itself, it's getting employees to actually change the way they perform their jobs in order to conform to standardized procedures. Unless you are willing to undertake a focused training program together with sustained managerial vigilance, you may not want to attempt the effort at all.

Unless your organization is relatively small, you should count on the installation and implementation of an ERP program to involve at least one year of effort. This minimum timeframe reflects the reality of factors such as installation, data conversion, data analysis, training, integration and testing, customization, add-ons, etc.

R*ecap*

Organizations establish techniques for forecasting their product-level needs based on the nature of the demand characteristics of those items.

Formulae for ensuring that you have the right item, in the right quantity, in the right place, at the right time can range from relatively simple min-max models to highly sophisticated computer-dependent systems.

For individuals not directly involved in purchasing, successful inventory control doesn't so much flow from actually using the various formulae, but rather from understanding what outcomes are supposed to result from their use.

ERP systems allow more efficient and effective operations throughout an enterprise by allowing all departments to have access to one another's data and information on a real-time basis.

REVIEW QUESTIONS

1. Independent demand is best described as:
    (a) erratic purchasing of inventory.
    (b) one item is needed because of its relationship to another item.
    (c) items are impacted by market conditions outside the control of your organization's operations, and they are therefore independent of operations.
    (d) demand for items outside of their normal review cycle.

2. Just-in-time manufacturing results in:
   (a) right item, right quantity, right place, right time.
   (b) right item, right quantity, right place.
   (c) right item, right quantity.
   (d) larger inventory levels.

3. Independent demand calls for a(n) _____ approach to inventory management.

4. Dependent demand calls for a(n) _____ approach to inventory management.

5. The reorder point is the
   (a) point in time when a product review is undertaken.
   (b) largest quantity of an item you will have on hand or on order.
   (c) lowest quantity of an item you will have on hand or on order before you reorder.
   (d) lowest quantity at which you can obtain a discount from a vendor.

6. The bill of materials is:
   (a) another name for a purchase order.
   (b) the recipe of raw materials and subassemblies that make up a finished product.
   (c) the schedule of what will be built, when, and in what quantities.
   (d) an accounts payable concept.

7. JIT systems regard inventory in excess of current production and R & D needs to be:
   (a) safety stock.

(b) FIFO inventory.

(c) waste.

(d) part of the kanban system.

8. True or False.
Enterprise Resource Planning software is developed for a single user's requirements.

(a) True

(b) False

Answers

1. (c), 2. (a), 3. replenishment, 4. requirements, 5. (c), 6. (b), 7. (c), 8. (b)

Note

1. This method of calculating the R Factor takes a straight average. It implies that every PO requires the same time and effort. Companies that calculate items using activity-based costing would probably develop the R Factor using a blended average.

CHAPTER 6

WHY INVENTORY SYSTEMS FAIL AND HOW TO FIX THEM

The objective of this chapter is to provide you with an understanding of the nature of inventory accuracy and the working tools to "fix" your inventory system. If all items are moving through a properly operating system, then it doesn't matter what the characteristics of an SKU are—expensive item, inexpensive item, fast mover, slow mover, long lead time, critical—the shelf count of the item (actual balance on-hand stock levels) and record count (how many your records say are supposed to be here) will match.

The traditional method of determining if actual balance on-hand stock levels match book/record levels is to take an annual physical inventory. As a method of correcting inventory accuracy problems, this costly and time-consuming effort is riddled with deficiencies. Why? Consider the following:

▸ Accuracy is often defined in dollars rather than in actual physical units. As discussed in Chapter 1, the dollar value of product does not reflect exactly what items are in-house. For example, imagine you sent out a thousand cases of peaches to a customer rather than the thousand cases of pears actually requested. An annual inventory would reflect an overall dollar value roughly equal to whatever it would have been even if the correct item had been shipped. Therefore, our shelf count is off a thousand over for one SKU and a thousand under for another with no discrepancy in accuracy—if accuracy is measured in dollars.

▶ Misidentification of product. As discussed in Chapter 3, product within a facility is misidentified for a variety of reasons. During annual inventories, misidentification often occurs because inexperienced counters assisting with the effort do not recognize items, misunderstand package descriptions, and so on.

▶ Misidentification of units of measure. Incorrect quantities are often written down during annual inventories because counters simply do not understand an SKU's pack size, pack size descriptions, or abbreviations on packaging.

▶ Discrepancies "adjusted away." Perhaps the greatest problem with using the annual inventory as a method for establishing accuracy is that it provides no method for backtracking through physical and paper transactions to determine why an item's shelf count and its record count do not agree—a 12-month time period is simply too long of an audit trail. Consequently, if the reason for a discrepancy cannot be immediately found during the inventory, an adjustment is made with the underlying cause of the error never being corrected.

At the end of an annual inventory, after all of the adjustments have been made and after the lights have been turned off, you have an inventory shelf and record count that agree. At least they agree until the next morning when the same system that spawned the discrepancies found during the effort reasserts itself and a new group of errors is born.

Albert Einstein, the famous physicist, once said, "A problem stated is a problem half-solved." Modern business writers like Peter Drucker have expressed a similar view, "A problem analyzed is a problem half-solved." The sentiment expressed in these sayings, that reviewing the nature of inventory problems is a key step in solving them, provides you with a good starting point in resolving your own inventory-related issues.

Inventory System Failure: A Case Example

The following events in this inventory system failure case example have been numbered for ease of reference. The events described in the case example characterize common misunderstandings between different operating units within an organization, as well as timing and sequencing disconnects in inventory movement and information capture that cause inventory systems to fail. The case example is followed by a discussion and explanation of each of the events described.

1. Big Hammer, Inc., manufactures and distributes widgets. Manufacturing occurs at its Los Angeles, CA, plant. It distributes from two separate locations. One of these locations is in Kansas City, MO, and has been part of Big Hammer for many years. The other location is in New York, NY, and is the surviving portion of Paulex Co., a distribution company just purchased by Big Hammer.

2. Marc, Big Hammer's president, has just reviewed operating reports from all three locations and is upset. It seems that the inventory accuracy level at all three locations is off. The end result

is delayed production, too much inventory, and poor customer service. In addition, various department heads in all three locations clash with one another. To straighten everything out, he hires the consulting firm of Alana, Eric, and Shawn.

3. Alana goes to KC. Eric goes to NY. Shawn goes to LA.

4. The trio immediately discovers that NY is using a different software system than LA and KC. In addition, the LA/KC software was designed for distribution, not manufacturing. However, some modifications have been made to the LA/KC software to help with manufacturing applications.

5. The NY system allocates inventory on a real-time basis. In other words, as a pick ticket is generated for an item, the quantity in question is allocated to a specific order and is not available for any other customer—its paper life ceases.

6. The LA/KC system is a batch system. Items are relieved from stock at the time the system is updated. This usually occurs once per day when billing is done. A modification to the system back-flushes[1] some items out of stock during the manufacturing cycle.

7. Eric wanders around the NY location and observes the following:

   7A. Salespeople, customer service personnel, clerical staff, and others freely roam through all stockrooms. Eric notices that some nonstockroom personnel fill their own orders, grab samples for customers, and put things back into the facility that they have previously removed.

   7B. Eric observes that some of these individuals document their actions immediately, while others document nothing, and others turn in necessary paperwork—later.

   7C. Eric observes Sally, a salesperson, peering intently at her computer screen. He hears her utter an oath and declare out loud, "I just saw a whole bunch of SKU #1234 out there a little while ago." She then creates a manual invoice within the software system, prints it, walks out into the stockroom, fills the order she has just created, delivers it to customer Acme Widgets of the World, and later drops the signed delivery copy on the desk of her accounts receivables clerk.

7D. Eric observes an angry exchange between the warehouse manager and the accounting manager of the NY location. They were arguing over a negative stock balance for SKU #1234.

7E. Eric also observes Sally angrily telling the warehouse manager that one of her customers, Widgets, Gidgets, Gadgets and Such, was shorted 10 widgets on an order it received "just a little while ago."

8. Alana has also observed some interesting things in KC.

8A. Alana has observed two different order fillers attempting to fill orders for the same item—from the same empty shelf.

8B. At 5 PM one evening, Alana was standing behind Carmen, the company's billing clerk. Carmen's inbox contained several inches of delivery slips ready for processing. Carmen got up and began to make preparations to go home. Alana asked her what she was doing. Carmen replied, "It's 5 PM, I'm going home."

Alana said, "But you still have a lot of work in your inbox."

"So what? I'll work on it tomorrow," Carmen indignantly responded.

"But you'll mess up the warehouse if you don't get those slips processed tonight," Alana stated.

Angrily, Carmen stated, "I work in accounting. I don't work in the warehouse."

Alana asked, "How long would it take you to do those?"

Carmen glanced at her inbox and replied, "About 30 minutes."

"Please stay and get them done," Alana cajoled.

"I can't even if I wanted to," Carmen said. "I'm not allowed any overtime."

Bill, one of Carmen's coworkers, chimes in and says, "Why can't you get your work done during the day?"

Furious, Carmen turns on Bill and says, "Hey, you sort and distribute the mail every morning, run photocopies of all incoming checks while fighting with people over our one copy machine, and prepare and go out to make the daily deposit like I do; and then let's see if you can get your stuff done."

8C. Hanging around the warehouse, Alana observed that receiving was done on a manual basis, and there wasn't always a copy of a PO in the warehouse to support incoming loads.

Alana noticed on several occasions that when receiving staff members did not have all appropriate paperwork for an item, they would simply put it away or move it off to the side. Then later, or the next day, they would hunt down all of the appropriate documentation and turn everything in to the data entry people for entry into the system.

Like Eric, Alana also observed nonstockroom individuals filling their own orders.

8D. Alana also observed a curious exchange between

Franklin, the accounting manager, and Carmen, the billing clerk.

While attempting to create an invoice for an item, Carmen's computer screen flashed an error message indicating that she was trying to bill for something that had a zero stock balance in the system. The software would not let her bill for an item it did not reflect as being available for the subject sale.

Carmen called Franklin over. She showed him the signed delivery slip indicating that the item had, in fact, been delivered.

Franklin stated, "Those people in the warehouse can't get anything right." He then proceeded to manually override the system and entered the SKU (SKU #4567) and quantity in question (10). Franklin then directed Carmen to try again. The invoice was created without any further problems.

Mid-morning of the next day, the stock records began to show that there were 10 of SKU #4567 in the facility. A telemarketing salesperson sold 10 SKU #4567s that afternoon. A pick ticket was generated for the order. The order filler could not find any of SKU #4567 in the warehouse. A stock adjustment form is processed to take these 10 items out of stock.

8E. Alana overhears a telephone conversation between Carmen and a customer. The customer wants to return five SKU #9876s and wants to ensure that it is not charged for them. Carmen notes the information, prepares a pickup slip, and issues a credit to the customer's account.

Later that day, a salesperson sells five SKU #9876's. A pick ticket was generated for the order. The order filler could not find any of SKU #9876s in the warehouse. A stock adjustment form is processed to take these five items out of stock.

9. Meanwhile, Shawn has been talking to Ichiro, the inventory control clerk in LA. Ichiro is frustrated. He works hard at his job but can't seem to track work in process.[2] Consequently, he is never sure how much of any particular item the company has available for production purposes.

10. Shawn observes a worker disassembling a subassembly. He asks the worker what he is doing. The worker replies that there is a rush order for which they lack all of the raw materials, so they are disassembling some less important assemblies to cannibalize the required parts.

Shawn asks if the products being disassembled are from other orders. The worker replies that they are. Shawn asks about any paperwork that was generated to support whatever it is the worker is doing. The worker replies that he doesn't know.

Set out below is a discussion and explanation of each of the events described above. For ease of reference, each event is restated and then followed by its debrief.

Discussion of Example Case

Event #1. Big Hammer, Inc., manufactures and distributes widgets. Manufacturing occurs at its Los Angeles, CA, plant. It distributes from two separate locations. One of these locations is in Kansas City, MO, and has been part of Big Hammer for many years. The other location is in New York, NY, and is the surviving portion of Paulex Co., a distribution company just purchased by Big Hammer.

Any organization that has several locations must clearly answer the "who, what, when, where, why, and how" questions: Who is doing what? When are they doing it? Where are they doing it? Why are they doing it? and How are they doing it? If these questions are not answered, materials and information will not flow smoothly between and among the organization's separate departments.

Event #2. Marc, Big Hammer's president, has just reviewed operating reports from all three locations and is upset. It seems that the inventory accuracy level at all three locations is off. The end result is delayed production, too much inventory, and poor customer service. In addition, various department heads in all three locations clash with one another. To straighten everything out, he hires the consulting firm of Alana, Eric, and Shawn.

Although consultants are helpful in most instances, by applying the concepts contained within this chapter, you should be able to resolve many system problems your organization may be currently experiencing.

Event #3. Alana goes to KC. Eric goes to NY. Shawn goes to LA.

Event #4. The trio immediately discovers that NY is using a different software system than LA and KC. In addition, the LA/KC software was designed for distribution, not manufacturing. However, some modifications have been made to the LA/KC software to help with manufacturing applications.

Trying to integrate different software systems is always difficult. Once again, any organization hoping to achieve that result must clearly lay out the timing and sequencing of the information flow within the system.

In addition, the demand patterns for items in a distribution world and those in a manufacturing environment are radically different. Purchasing patterns for finished goods and spare parts in a distribution are based on past usage patterns. Purchasing patterns for the raw materials and subassemblies used in manufacturing are based on the master production schedule. Different concepts and formulae are used for each type of inventory and, therefore, software designed for one or the other or specifically written for a combination environment should be used whenever possible.

Event #5. *The NY system allocates inventory on a real-time basis. In other words, as a pick ticket is generated for an item, the quantity in question is allocated to a specific order and is not available for any other customer—its paper life ceases.*

The central problem often encountered in real-time systems is that there is often a time lapse between the creation of a pick ticket and the actual removal of the product from the shelves.

Since the items on the pick ticket were immediately allocated[3] to that order, with their paper life ceasing, those SKUs will actually be sitting on the shelves but won't appear in the then current record count.

Somewhere in the software files is the information: total items on hand, items allocated, and items actually available for sale or use. The problem is that not everyone in the organization has access to this information! If (a) staff members are allowed to fill their own orders and (b) do not understand how it is possible to check the then current stock records and see a lower number of items than are actually sitting in plain view, then (c) they will stop believing in the record count, will only believe their eyes, and will raid product allocated for other orders.

Event #6. *The LA/KC system is a batch system. Items are relieved from stock at the time the system is updated. This usually occurs once per day when billing is done. A modification to the system backflushes[1] some items out of stock during the manufacturing cycle.*

The most significant issue created by batch software systems is that items are physically gone from the shelves/building but still appear in the record count until the system is updated. The longer the length of time between updates, the more out of balance the shelf count and the record count are. Backflushing works well if the backflush occurs at each level of the bill of materials. See the discussion of Event #9.

Event #7. *Eric wanders around the NY location and observes what follows in Event #8.*

Event #8. *Salespeople, customer service personnel, clerical staff, and others freely roam through all stockrooms. Eric notices that some nonstockroom personnel fill their own orders, grab samples for customers, and put things back into the facility that they have previously removed.*

Any organization hoping to always have its shelf count match its record count simply must stop all unauthorized personnel from touching anything in a stockroom or warehouse. In addition, authorized personnel must have a paper- or computer-based document before placing anything into or removing anything from storage areas. These points cannot be overstated. They are imperative to inventory accuracy.

Event #9. *Eric observes that some of these individuals document their actions immediately, while others document nothing, and others turn in necessary paperwork—later.*

Documentation created after something has been placed into or removed from a facility creates all sorts of problems. For example:

a. If an item is physically removed without a document deleting it from inventory, then salespeople, production schedulers, and others will believe that the item is still available for sale or use. They will then generate pick tickets for its selection.

Order fillers will then waste their time looking for items that do not exist. The order fillers will generate adjustment forms leading to the items being deleted from inventory. Eventually, when the original documentation goes through the system, it causes these same items to be deleted from inventory—again. Your shelf count and record count are now almost hopelessly out of balance.

b. If an item is placed into the stockroom without accompanying paperwork, then the subject SKU is unavailable for sale or use—since no one knows it's there.

Event #10. *Eric observes Sally, a salesperson, peering intently at her computer screen. He hears her utter an oath and declare out loud, "I just saw a whole bunch of SKU #1234 out there a little while ago." She then creates a manual invoice within the software system, prints it, walks out into the stockroom, fills the order she has just created, delivers it to customer Acme Widgets of the World, and later drops the signed delivery copy on the desk of her accounts receivables clerk.*

Event #10 is an example of someone in a real-time software scenario who does not understand how it is possible to have a stock record (in the computer or on hard paper copy) that reflects a stock balance lower than the actual number of items on the shelves. Recall that the discrepancy is due to the time period between the creation of a pick ticket with its allocation of product to an order and the physical removal of the SKUs from the stockroom.

Event #11. *Eric observes an angry exchange between the warehouse manager and the accounting manager of the NY location. They were arguing over a negative stock balance for SKU #1234.*

Since this is a real-time system, when Sally created a manual pick ticket she caused the system to allocate and delete the subject SKU. If the stock balance was zero when Sally did this, her actions have caused the balance to go into a negative.

As discussed in Event #7 of this section, Sally's actions have also created the potential for a much different problem in an entirely different department of the organization. By forcing a manual invoice through the system and dropping off a delivery slip for billing, Sally has created the potential for a billing clerk to try to create an invoice for product that the system has never received into itself. Many accounting programs will not let an invoice be created for product that has never been received.

Event #12. Eric also observes Sally angrily telling the warehouse manager that one of her customers, Widgets, Gidgets, Gadgets and Such, was shorted 10 widgets on an order it received "just a little while ago."

In Event #7C it should be obvious that the product Sally took had already been allocated to a different customer (Customer #1) than the one she was taking care of at that time (Customer #2). Sally's actions caused her to raid Customer #1's order, causing a stockout for one of her own customers—Customer #1.

Event #13. Alana has also observed some interesting things in KC.

Event #14. Alana has observed two different order fillers attempting to fill orders for the same item—from the same empty shelf.

It is common in batch systems that are only updated once per day and in which there is no way to easily check (without going to look) the availability of an item for multiple orders to be written against the same "phantom" items. This also creates the danger of multiple adjustments adding to the overall confusion.

Event #15. At 5 PM one evening, Alana was standing behind Carmen, the company's billing clerk. Carmen's inbox contained several inches of delivery slips ready for processing. Carmen got up and began to make preparations to go home. Alana asked her what she was doing. Carmen replied, "It's 5 PM, I'm going home."

Alana said, "But you still have a lot of work in your inbox."

"So what? I'll work on it tomorrow," Carmen indignantly responded.

"But you'll mess up the warehouse if you don't get those slips processed tonight," Alana stated.

Angrily, Carmen stated, "I work in accounting. I don't work in the warehouse."

Alana asked, "How long would it take you to do those?"

Carmen glanced at her inbox and replied, "About 30 minutes."

"Please stay and get them done," Alana cajoled.

"I can't even if I wanted to," Carmen said. "I'm not allowed any overtime."

Bill, one of Carmen's coworkers, chimes in and says, "Why can't you get your work done during the day?"

Furious, Carmen turns on Bill and says, "Hey, you sort and distribute the mail every morning, run photocopies of all incoming checks while fighting with people over our one copy machine, and prepare and go out to make the daily deposit like I do; and then let's see if you can get your stuff done."

A number of issues are raised by the Event #15 scenario, including:

a. The morning following an incident like the one described will find everyone who deals with inventory—sales, accounting, production scheduling, customer service, and purchasing—making decisions on information they believe is as current as of the night before when the system was updated. The reality is that the information is no more current than the last time Carmen made it to the bottom of the inbox. If she hasn't made it to the bottom of her basket in several days, then the records and operations are really suffering.

The problem is compounded by the fact that roughly 20 percent of our inventory will represent 80 percent of our most important items. Therefore, not only does our shelf count not match our record count, but they don't match regarding some of our most important items.

b. Another problem revealed by the incident is that the organization does not recognize the importance of getting all receiving and shipping into and out of the building on both a real-life and paper-life basis every day. This is indicated by those duties assigned to Carmen that cause her not to complete her inventory-related tasks on a daily basis. Although these duties are important, they should be performed by someone whose actions do not have the ripple effect that Carmen's actions have throughout the entire organization.

Event #16. *Hanging around the warehouse, Alana observed that receiving was done on a manual basis, and there wasn't always a copy of a PO in the warehouse to support incoming loads.*

Alana noticed on several occasions that when the receiving staff members did not have all appropriate paperwork for an item, they would simply put it away or move it off to the side. Then later, or the next day, they would hunt down all of the appropriate documentation and turn everything in to the data entry people for entry into the system.

Like Eric, Alana also observed nonstockroom individuals filling their own orders.

Virtually every organization has a purchase order system. And, in virtually every organization, anyone with the authority to buy something is repeatedly told to have a PO for everything. In spite of those facts, in many organizations product comes in daily without any supporting documentation. This causes confusion, inefficient receiving operations, and separates an item's real life from its paper life. (See also Chapter 1.) There should be either a hard copy or a record of the PO in the computer system available to receiving for all items that arrive at the stockroom.

When an item's real life becomes separated from its paper life, people begin to ship or use product that has not been received; to put away product that has not been received so that no one knows it is available for sale or use creates an environment where inventory clerks and accounting personnel are making adjustment after adjustment to the record count.

Event #17. Alana also observed a curious exchange between Franklin, the accounting manager, and Carmen, the billing clerk.

While attempting to create an invoice for an item, Carmen's computer screen flashed an error message indicating that she was trying to bill for something that had a zero stock balance in the system. The software would not let her bill for an item it did not reflect as being available for the subject sale.

Carmen called Franklin over. She showed him the signed delivery slip indicating that the item had, in fact, been delivered.

Franklin stated, "Those people in the warehouse can't get anything right." He then proceeded to manually override the system and entered the SKU (SKU #4567) and quantity in question (10). Franklin then directed Carmen to try again. The invoice was created without any further problems.

Mid-morning of the next day, the stock records began to show that there were 10 of SKU #4567 in the facility. A telemarketing salesperson sold 10 SKU #4567s that afternoon. A pick ticket was generated for the order. The order filler could not find any of SKU #4567 in the warehouse. A stock adjustment form is processed to take these 10 items out of stock.

From Event #16, it appears here that someone delivered an item that had not yet gone through the paperwork receiving cycle. Then when Carmen tried to bill for it, the software would not let her.

Instead of researching what had actually happened, Franklin overrode the system and put in a quantity of 10. Carmen's billing then deleted the 10 items.

When the receiving paperwork finally made it through the system it created a quantity of 10 items that were no longer in the building. These 10 phantom items were then sold—maybe more than once.

When the 10 items could not be found, additional paperwork had to be initiated to delete the SKUs from the system.

All of the above issues are caused, in part, by a lack of understanding on the part of various staff members of how the timing and sequencing of the system works.

Event #18. *Alana overhears a telephone conversation between Carmen and a customer. The customer wants to return five SKU #9876s and wants to ensure that it is not charged for them. Carmen notes the information, prepares a pickup slip, and issues a credit to the customer's account.*

Later that day, a salesperson sells five SKU #9876's. A pick ticket was generated for the order. The order filler could not find any of SKU #9876s in the warehouse. A stock adjustment form is processed to take these five items out of stock.

Although application software systems vary widely in how items are accounted for, many systems place an item back into stock (in the database) when a credit is issued against that item. By issuing a credit, Carmen caused the software system to place the five SKUs back into stock—even though they had not yet been returned to the building.

Again, a lack of understanding regarding timing and sequencing of software and events causes terrible dysfunctions to stockroom operations.

Event #19. Meanwhile, Shawn has been talking to Ichiro, the inventory control clerk in LA. Ichiro is frustrated. He works hard at his job but can't seem to track work in process.[2] Consequently, he is never sure how much of any particular item the company has available for production purposes.

As indicated in Event #4, a key problem Ichiro faces is that the company is using two separate methods of relieving items from stock. One method is batch, while the other is a backflush of some items. Recall that backflushing refers to a software technique where raw materials and other components going into a particular subassembly or final product are relieved from stock when that subassembly/product is completed.

As indicated in the discussion of Event #6, if a batch system is not updated with some degree of frequency, it is difficult to understand what is available without actually looking. This problem can be overcome through software modules that advise the stockkeeper of those SKUs that have gone into completed orders. This report shows a running total for each SKU that has been drawn down that day. Once the system is updated, then a new report begins.

The key issue regarding backflushing is whether the backflush occurs at every level of the bill of materials. See Exhibit 6–1. (A similar example is also used in Exhibit 5–4.) If the backflush only goes down one level, but no backflush occurred at that next lower level, then all materials below that level will still appear to be in stock. In reality they have been used up.

Event #20. Shawn observes a worker disassembling a subassembly. He asks the worker what he is doing. The worker replies that there is a

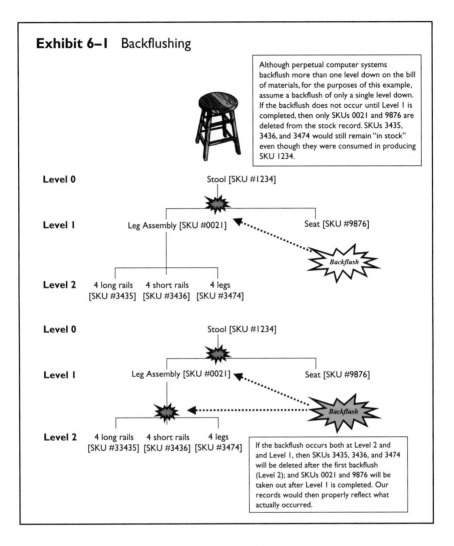

Exhibit 6–1 Backflushing

Although perpetual computer systems backflush more than one level down on the bill of materials, for the purposes of this example, assume a backflush of only a single level down. If the backflush does not occur until Level 1 is completed, then only SKUs 0021 and 9876 are deleted from the stock record. SKUs 3435, 3436, and 3474 would still remain "in stock" even though they were consumed in producing SKU 1234.

Level 0 Stool [SKU #1234]

Level 1 Leg Assembly [SKU #0021]   Seat [SKU #9876]

Backflush

Level 2 4 long rails   4 short rails   4 legs
[SKU #3435]   [SKU #3436]   [SKU #3474]

Level 0 Stool [SKU #1234]

Level 1 Leg Assembly [SKU #0021]   Seat [SKU #9876]

Backflush

Level 2 4 long rails   4 short rails   4 legs
[SKU #33435]   [SKU #3436]   [SKU #3474]

If the backflush occurs both at Level 2 and and Level 1, then SKUs 3435, 3436, and 3474 will be deleted after the first backflush (Level 2); and SKUs 0021 and 9876 will be taken out after Level 1 is completed. Our records would then properly reflect what actually occurred.

rush order for which they lack all of the raw materials, so they are disassembling some less important assemblies to cannibalize the required parts.

Shawn asks if the products being disassembled are from other orders. The worker replies that they are. Shawn asks about any paperwork that was generated to support whatever it is the worker is doing. The worker replies that he doesn't know.

Metrics

"You can't control what you don't measure."

—Peter Drucker

Before doing *anything* toward establishing methods to discover, analyze, and fix any discrepancies between actual on-hand stock levels and database record levels, you should take a snapshot of where you are *now*. There are two sets of numbers you should develop that relate to (a) *inventory record accuracy (IRA)* and (b) *fill rate*.

IRA is a reflection of how well your shelf count and record count match. In other words, do your stock records accurately reflect what is actually in the stockroom?

Fill rate is a reflection of how effective your inventory is. Did you have what you needed when you needed it?

INVENTORY RECORD ACCURACY

An excellent way to establish a benchmark of how accurate your inventory records are "right now" is to take a test count.

Test Counting

A quick, accurate method of establishing your current IRA is to perform a test count:

▶ Select 100 SKUs that represent a cross-section of all items. In other words, select all sorts of items—fast movers, slow movers, expensive items, inexpensive items, and those with both long and short lead times to acquire.

▶ Count all 100 in all locations where they are located. Measure accuracy by considering actual units on the floor—not dollar value.

▶ Divide the number of accurate counts by the total number of counts. Accurate counts mean where the record count and the shelf count exactly match.

▶ Quotient is your inventory record accuracy. See Exhibit 6–2.

Exhibit 6–2 Test Counting to Establish Inventory Record Accuracy

$$\frac{\text{Accurate Counts}}{\text{Total Counts}} = \frac{\text{Inventory Record Accuracy}}{} \quad \frac{87}{100} = .87 = 87\% \text{ IRA}$$

Tolerances

How accurate does accuracy have to be? You may think, at first, that accurate means that 100 percent of the time your stock records match your shelf counts. Consider, however, your feelings about counting a large container of nails.

In counting a large container of nails, would you actually count each nail individually? It is more probable that you will (a) weigh out one pound of nails, (b) count the number of nails in a pound, (c) weigh all of the nails, and (d) then compute the total number of nails by comparing the number of nails in a pound to the number of pounds of nails in the container. Will your computation capture the exact number of nails in the container? Probably not. Do you really care? Probably not. Why? Because of the nature of the SKU in question, in this case nails, is low cost, easy to acquire, and hard to count individually (if there is a large quantity of them). Therefore, you would probably be willing to accept some percentage of tolerance in your numbers. If you were within ±5 percent of a perfect match between the record count and the shelf count, would you be satisfied? Probably so. Would you be equally satisfied applying the same approach to a large container of diamonds? Of course not.

Many organizations allow a variance or tolerance in considering IRA. That is, they allow a plus-minus percentage of accuracy they find acceptable. These tolerances can be set using dollars, actual units, or some combination of the two. Most accountants use dollars. Stockkeepers should use actual units: It's either here or it isn't.

Few organizations accept a tolerance of greater than ±5 percent on any item. In other words, a 95 percent tolerance should be the lowest variance from a 100 percent accuracy level you will accept for any item no matter what its characteristics.

If you will accept tolerances, they must be set for each item or category of item with great care. Consider the following factors:

▸ Dollar value: The higher the dollar value, the more accuracy you will demand.

▸ Usage rate: Usage rate can actually be argued in two ways:

- The Higher-the-Usage-Rate-the-Lower-the-Tolerance-Level Argument: If you are using a large quantity of an item, you will want to always know how much is available so there is never a stockout.

- The Lower-the-Usage-Rate-Lower-the-Tolerance-Level Argument: If an item is not moving very quickly, then why should there be any discrepancy between shelf and record count? A low variance percentage for a slow-moving item will alert everyone to a problem quickly, as opposed to waiting for a crisis. This argument assumes that if there are stockouts on higher-moving products, then the situation will alert everyone anyway.

▸ Lead time: The longer the lead time, the lower the tolerance level. A long lead time requires more working reserve and safety stock. See also Chapter 5.

▶ Level on bill of materials: The higher something is on the bill of materials, the more overall value it has. Therefore, the higher on the bill of materials an SKU is, the lower the tolerance.

▶ Criticality: Some items are critical for reasons other than dollar value, usage rate, or lead time. A safety equipment company may only sell a few biohazard cleanup suits per year, but when they are needed they are needed immediately.

▶ Combination of the above

In the following scenario, you'll find an example of considering tolerances.

Melvin, President of Megawatts, Inc., doesn't believe in allowing any tolerances in his inventory levels. His friend, Sarah, President of Bright Lights Co., does.

A cross-section of 100 items was counted in each of these companies' facilities.

The actual stock count on 87 SKUs in each facility matched the respective companies' stock records.

Bright Lights allowed a variance of ±2 percent on 5 of the 13 items that were not 100 percent accurate. The count of these 5 fell within their respective tolerances.

$$\text{Megawatts:} \quad \frac{87}{100} = 87\% \text{ accuracy}$$

$$\text{Bright Lights:} \quad \frac{92}{100} = 92\% \text{ accuracy}$$

Melvin argues that Sarah's higher IRA level is artificial and doesn't really reflect accuracy.

Sarah's approach does reflect an acceptable level of accuracy if the tolerances were carefully set. As in the container of nails example, if we (1) weighed a large container of nails and determined there were 14,003 nails, (2) entered that total into our records, (3) reweighed the nails and determined there were 14,010 nails, would we change our records? Probably not. The second total would fall within an acceptable tolerance.

Once you have set tolerances, you should not make adjustments to your records when a discrepancy between shelf and record counts falls within the variance allowed. If an item does fall outside of the tolerance range, you would hunt down the reason for the discrepancy and adjust the record if necessary. See Exhibit 6–3.

FILL RATES

Although matching shelf count to record count is one way of measuring inventory, it does not indicate if you have the items you need when you need them. Simple fill rate calculations achieve that objective. The fill rate looks at the qualitative nature of your inventory efforts.

Fill Rate Formulae

Simple Fill Rate:

$$\text{Fill Rate} = \frac{\text{Items Shipped on a Given Day}}{\text{Items Ordered for Shipment on a Given Day}} \quad \frac{417 \text{ Items Shipped}}{447 \text{ Items Ordered}} = 0.93 = 93\% \text{ Fill Rate}$$

The above indicates that you had 93 percent of the items you needed on the day they were required.

The fill rate can reflect the availability of a single item or a grouping of items.

Exhibit 6–3 Tolerances and Adjustments

Assume that a count was made of 10 SKUs, with the results being as follows:

SKU	RECORD COUNT	ACTUAL COUNT	% DEVIATION	% TOLERANCE	HIT/MISS
1	1,200	1,128	−6%	2%	M
2	2,217	2,106	−5%	5%	H
3	317	304	−4%	5%	H
4	8,947	8,679	−3%	2%	M
5	100	98	−2%	5%	H
6	567	561	−1%	2%	H
7	100	100	0%	0%	H
8	1,367	1,381	+1%	0%	M
9	1,432	1,461	+2%	2%	H
10	185	191	+3%	5%	H

SKUs 1, 4, and 8 fell outside of their tolerances. For example, if the count for SKU 1 would have fallen within the range of 1,176 to 1,224, ±2 percent of the record count, then it would have been a hit. It was not. Therefore, you would research why the discrepancies exist and adjust your records if necessary.

All of the other SKUs fell within their tolerances. However, only SKU 7 was exactly correct. You would still not make any adjustments to any SKUs where there was a hit. The variance percentages you set should allow you a comfortable range in which you can tolerate some up or down differences. Often pluses and minuses cancel one another out over time.

Stockouts Per Year:

$$\text{Stockout \%} = \frac{\substack{\text{Number of Days} \\ \text{Where all Orders Were} \\ \text{Not Shipped Complete}}}{\substack{\text{Total Number of} \\ \text{Shipping Days} \\ \text{During the Year}}} \quad \frac{34}{200^4} = 0.17 = 17\%$$

This indicates that you were unable to send all orders out complete 17 percent of the time. Stated more positively, you were able to send orders out complete 83 percent of the time.

Tools with Which to Uncover System Dysfunctions

To solve problems you need to engage in:

▶ Fact finding—what is happening now?

▶ Problem finding—what is wrong with what is going on?

▶ Solution finding—how can we fix what is wrong?

So far this chapter has focused on (a) beginning to analyze inventory problems in an intellectual, intuitive, "gut feel" manner, and (b) developing some measurements with which to understand your current level of inventory accuracy and availability. This is part of fact finding.

Another way of determining what is actually happening at your facility is to create a number of charts.

Charts, by their very nature, allow you to analyze things. However, you need to guard against "paralysis by analysis." If everything is equally important, then nothing is important. In other words, you should only chart things that are really important to controlling inventory items, trends, operational undertakings, and so on.

RUN CHARTS

Run charts allow you to measure a variable that changes over time.

A run chart is an *x–y* axis chart with the unit of measure appearing on the vertical *y*-axis, and the timeframe running along the horizontal *x*-axis. The unit of measure can be anything you wish to track such as stockouts, errors, labor hours, pieces, pounds, or gallons. The timeframe can also be whatever you desire it to be such as seconds, minutes, hours, days, weeks, months, or years. See Exhibit 6–4.

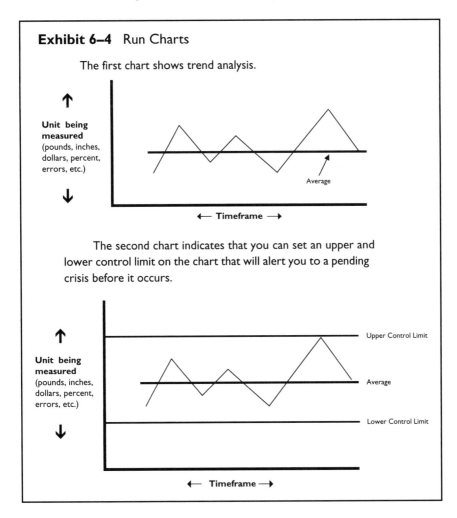

Exhibit 6–4 Run Charts

The first chart shows trend analysis.

Unit being measured (pounds, inches, dollars, percent, errors, etc.)

Average

← Timeframe →

The second chart indicates that you can set an upper and lower control limit on the chart that will alert you to a pending crisis before it occurs.

Unit being measured (pounds, inches, dollars, percent, errors, etc.)

Upper Control Limit

Average

Lower Control Limit

← Timeframe →

FLOW CHARTS

Flow charts allow you to analyze the sequence of a set of events. A flow chart does not necessarily show the interdependence of events or which events are going on at the same time as others.

Flow charts are easier to understand than written procedures.

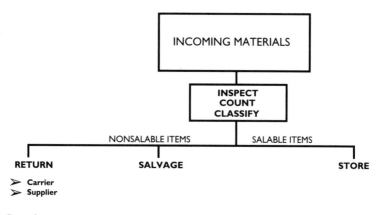

Caution:

▶ You do not have to use traditional flow chart symbols. Be consistent, however, with the symbols you do use or you will confuse yourself and others. Provide a key to symbols.

▶ Have version control. If flow charts are not revised as procedures change, they are worthless.

LOGIC CHARTS

Logic charts are flow charts that show the interrelationships of events.

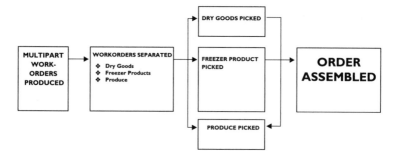

VARIANCE REPORTS

Variance reports compare an expectation with what actually occurred.

Variance reports can be based on any factor necessary for tracking an expectation. Some factors are dollars, labor, consumption rates, lines/pieces per hour, or trucks per day.

VARIANCE REPORT				
DESCRIPTION	PROJECTED	ACTUAL	VARIANCE AMOUNT	PERCENT
TOTAL				

Cycle Counting

After becoming familiar with your system through utilization of the techniques described in this chapter, you should be ready to systematically approach "fixing" whatever might be causing discrepancies between your shelf and record counts.

The most systematic method of solving inventory problems and enjoying a consistently high IRA is cycle counting. Cycle counting is simply counting a statistically significant cross-section of your inventory frequently.

This continuous counting leads to the discovery of discrepancies soon after they arise. By catching an error quickly, you can backtrack through both the paperwork and the stock movement of the item(s) to determine why that SKU's paper life became separated from its real life. Once the cause of the error is identified, it can be eliminated.

Since this is a continuous process, as one cause of error after another is eliminated the system begins to operate more and more smoothly. Eventually all items move through a series of procedures that work.

Cycle counting is different than an annual inventory in several ways.

ANNUAL INVENTORIES
In a nutshell, the objective of an annual physical inventory is to satisfy an accounting need.

Objectives:

▶ The objective of the annual physical inventory is to produce a financial valuation of the inventory on a given day.

▶ Every item must be counted as part of the annual inventory.

The 12-month-long audit trail of the annual physical is too long for any serious effort made at uncovering why an error occurred or even when—did it happen yesterday, last month, 10 months ago?

CYCLE COUNTING
In a nutshell, the objective of cycle counting is to identify and correct system failures that result in inaccurate inventory records.

Objectives:

▶ Discover discrepancies soon after they occur

▶ Identify causes of errors

▶ Correct conditions causing errors

▶ Continuous process improvement

▶ Minimum of 95 percent accuracy on ALL items

▶ Correct statement of inventory assets

Eliminate annual inventory. Most accounting firms will allow an organization to stop taking annual physical inventories once the company has established a mature cycle counting program. Generally, a company will cycle-count for at least 12 months. Then, an annual physical inventory is taken and the numbers from the annual are compared with the cycle count figures. If they match, then in the future the accounting firm will merely test-count once per year for valuation purposes.

Not every item in the building has to be counted as part of a cycle count, only a statistically significant cross-section of all items.

CYCLE COUNT METHODOLOGIES

There are a number of cycle count methodologies.

- ▶ Control Group
- ▶ Location Audit
- ▶ Random Selection
- ▶ Diminishing Population
- ▶ Product Categories
- ▶ A-B-C Categorization

A key point to remember is that no matter what cycle count methodology you eventually choose to follow, when you first begin and your inventory record accuracy is low, you will not count a large number of items per day. This is because it will take time to recount, review paperwork, talk to people, and do all of the other things necessary to determine why an item's record count and shelf count do not match. Why count 50 items a day if you can only count and reconcile 10 of them? As your record accuracy increases, and more and more items match their record counts, you can comfortably count more items each day.

Any cycle count methodology will assist you in achieving high levels of IRA. However, not every method works in every company setting. For example:

Assumptions:

▶ You wish to cycle-count each item four times per year

▶ Cycle-count 200 days per year (4 days/wk × 50 wks = 200 count days)[4] 10,000 SKUs

▶ Three cycle counters working 7 hours per day

▶ Company A has 10,000 items that are unitized and in single locations within the stockroom

▶ It takes Company A an average of 2 minutes to count an item

Company B has 10,000 items that are not unitized, would have to be counted in "onesy-twosy," and each item is found in multiple locations throughout the facility

It takes Company B an average of 5 minutes to count an item

Company A	Company B
10,000 SKUs × 4 counts/yr = 40,000 counts	10,000 SKUs × 4 counts/yr = 40,000 counts
40,000 counts ÷ 200 days = 200 counts/day	40,000 counts ÷ 200 days = 200 counts/day
200 counts/day × 2 minutes = 400 minutes	200 counts/day × 5 minutes = 1,000 minutes
400 minutes ÷ 60 minutes = 7 hours/day	1,000 minutes ÷ 60 minutes = 17 hours/day
7 hours/day ÷ 3 counters = 2.33 hours/day each	17 hours/day ÷ 3 counters = 6 hours/day each

Treating all items equally and counting them four times per year *may* work for Company A, but it seems an unreasonable burden for Company B.

You should select a method that fits your own organization's resources and inventory types.

CONTROL GROUP CYCLE COUNTING METHOD

No matter which method you eventually decide to use, always start with a small-scale counting test run. By using a control group approach you will be able to:

▶ Immediately identify significant system problems, such as unrestricted access to the stockroom, major timing problems related to when product is moved, and when records of the move are updated.

▶ Develop an understanding of the who, what, when, where, why, and how of the way your system actually works.

▶ When you first begin cycle counting you will probably make adjustments only to find that you made a mistake. It is much simpler to correct errors related to only a few SKUs rather than hundreds of them.

Control Group Procedure

Set out below is a step-by-step procedure for using a control group to teach yourself basic cycle counting techniques.

▶ Select 100 items as a control group. IMPORTANT: The SKUs selected must be a true cross-section of the entire population of items they represent, such as some expensive items, some inexpensive, some fast movers, some slow, or some with a long lead time, etc.

▶ Count only 10 items per day. Use a Control Group Count Tracking Sheet. See Exhibit 6–5.

▶ Count for 100 days.

▶ Stats: $10 \times 100 = 1,000$ counts

▶ "Cycle" is 10 days

▶ Each item counted 10 times during test

Exhibit 6–5 Control Group Count Tracking Sheet

	SKU #	DESCRIPTION	1	2	3	4	5	6	7	8	9	10
1	BD79	Widget	✓	✓								
2	QD455	Gidget	✓	✓								
3	XD110	Gadget	✓	✓								
4	PD418	Thig-a-ma-jig	✓	✓								
5	AC123	Doohickey	✓	✓								
6	ZG23	Receiver	✓	✓								
97	HG786	Receiver Mount	✓									
98	LK951	Miniplexer	✓									
99	LK236	Multiplexer	✓									
100	DK47	Radome	✓									

Because you have tracked the same items over and over again, at the conclusion of your control group cycle count you should be able to eliminate major systems problems and have a good understanding of how your overall inventory system is working.

The control group approach should only be used as a starting point and not as an ongoing cycle count method. The reason for this is that the control group is not statistically large enough to actually represent your entire inventory.

Now you are ready to select a cycle count method that best suits your own organization's needs.

LOCATION AUDIT CYCLE COUNTING METHOD

In this approach, you divide the stockroom(s) up in some logical method—rooms, racks, bins, and so on. See Exhibit 6–6. Then on each counting day you count the SKUs found in those areas.

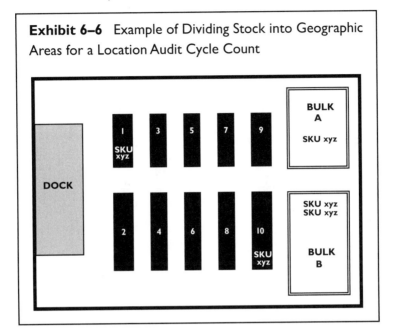

Exhibit 6–6 Example of Dividing Stock into Geographic Areas for a Location Audit Cycle Count

All items are treated equally. In other words, selection of those items included on that day's count is based solely on the item being located in the area counted. No other characteristics, such as cost, usage rate, and so on, are considered.

The length of the cycle depends on how many areas are to be counted. For example, if you were counting by rack, one rack per day, and there were 45 racks, then the entire cycle would be 45 days. You would then start over again.

The location audit approach has two significant benefits:

1. This approach does not require detailed recordkeeping of whether or not you have counted a specific item or the exact number of times you have counted it. It is administratively simple to follow.

2. This approach serves as a double audit because you are checking the quantity of an item at the same time that you are checking

to make sure it is in the right location in your facility. Product that has been misplaced can be "discovered" sooner than the annual inventory through the use of this method.

Two separate approaches are possible regarding how much of any selected SKU gets counted:

1. Only count the SKU in the location being cycle-counted that day.

   Example: Count only the quantity of SKU xyz in Rack 1. See Exhibit 6–6. Item xyz located in Rack 10 and in both bulk storage areas are ignored.

   This first approach requires a higher level of sophistication within your own inventory control system. Your system must allow you to identify not only how much of an item you have, but also each location it is located in and how much of it is in each location. See also Chapter 3, Physical Location and Control of Inventory.

   This first approach forces you to keep your shelf count and record count accurate on an ongoing basis.

2. Count the selected SKU in all locations where it may be located throughout the facility.

   Example: Quantities of SKU xyz counted in Racks 1 and 10 and in both bulk areas.

   With either locational audit approach, the warehouse will be counted wall to wall during the cycle. However, this does not mean that all items in the stockroom during that cycle will actually be counted.

   Not all items in the stockroom during the cycle will be counted because items will arrive into and leave from areas already counted or to be counted during the cycle. In other words, SKUs will be coming in behind you and moving away from in front of you as you go through the count. Does it matter if every item in the stockroom is counted during a location audit cycle? It does not matter that all items are not counted during any particular cycle because of the large number of items that are counted during that cycle. Remember that in cycle counting, you are interested in looking at the system, not individual SKUs within the system. Whether or not a SKU's shelf and record counts match is merely a way of determining if the system is actually working. Therefore, as long as you count a statistically significant number of the total items in the stockroom, you will accomplish the cycle count objective.

RANDOM SELECTION CYCLE COUNTING METHOD

This is probably the easiest form of cycle counting. The items selected for counting are totally random. However, the SKUs selected must be a true cross-section of the entire population of items they represent: some expensive items, some inexpensive, some fast movers, some slow movers, some with a long lead time.

The cycle is generally one year with a statistically significant number of SKUs being counted during that timeframe. For example,

- 10,000 total SKUs
- 200 counting days
- Therefore, 50 items/day counted $(10,000 \div 200 = 50)$
- 10,000 total counts during the year—a statistically significant number!

All items are treated equally. Product characteristics like dollar value and usage rate are ignored.

DIMINISHING POPULATION CYCLE COUNTING METHOD

This is a versatile approach. It can be used as a stand-alone procedure or used as part of the product category approach or the A-B-C approach, which are both explained later in this chapter.

    The basic concept is to:

1. Count each item in a defined population before counting any item over again.

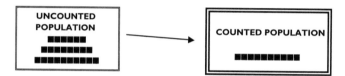

2. Then you begin the count all over again.

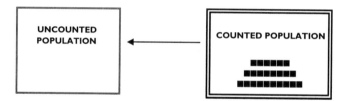

    The diminishing population technique ensures all items in the population are counted at least once per cycle.

    The number of times the total population is counted during a year depends on the size of the total number of items there are and how many days you are willing to count. See Exhibit 6–7.

    The larger the number of items counted per day the more cycles can be completed during the year.

PRODUCT CATEGORIES CYCLE COUNTING METHOD

To this point in our cycle count discussion, we have ignored an item's characteristics. In the product categories approach, the organization decides on what categories it wishes to place SKUs into based on some characteristics, such as by manufacturer or by type of use (the "criteria").

Items matching the criteria are counted either on the basis of:

(a) a single even (e.g., only items whose balance-on-hand equals zero), or

(b) using the diminishing population technique for each separate category: all of the widgets this week, all of the gadgets next week, all of the gidgets the week after, and so on.

The number of items to be counted can vary or be set by the number of items in the group divided by the number of days in the cycle. See Exhibit 6–7.

Cycle can be a single day or a defined number of times per year.

Exhibit 6–7 Diminishing Population Cycle Counting

EXAMPLE:	EXAMPLE:	EXAMPLE:
• 900 total SKUs	• 900 total SKUs	• 900 total SKUs
• 200 counting days in cycle	• 100 counting days in cycle	• 50 counting days in cycle
• $900 \div 200$ $= 4.5 > 5$ items/day	• 2 cycles per year	• 4 cycles per year
• 1,000 total counts/yr	• $900 \div 100$ $= 9$ items/day	• $900 \div 50$ $= 18$ items/day
	• 1,800 total counts/yr	• 3,600 total counts/yr

Single Criteria

You should be careful of using single event characteristics in defining categories. For example:

Criteria: Only cycle-count items on that day's purchase orders.

Benefits:

1. Ensures that correct quantity is being ordered.
2. Allows for count when stock level is at a low point. Makes it easier to count.

Problems:

a. Only the fastest moving items receive attention. Expensive but slower use items might be ignored until there is a crisis.
b. A true cross-section of all types of SKUs won't be represented until a large part of the year will have past and when POs for most items will have been written and released.
c. Ignores completely items that are not ordered during a given year such as where the quantity on hand exceeds your use for that entire year.

Criteria: Only cycle-count items at zero or negative balance

Benefits:

1. Negative balances should always trigger a count.
2. Items at zero should be easy to verify.

Problems:

a. Neither of these is statistically significant and both fail to represent a cross-section of all items.

Using the Diminishing Population Technique with Product Categories

▶ Define the criteria by which each SKU will be placed into a category.

▶ Decide sequence in which categories will be counted: all manufacturer X's products this week, all of manufacturer Y's products next week.

▶ Divide the number of SKUs in the category by the number of days to determine how many must be counted per day. See Exhibit 6–7.

▶ Move to the next category.

The product categories method of cycle counting involves a great deal of administration but provides you with more detailed information and audit trails as to what you have actually done during a cycle count.

A-B-C ANALYSIS CYCLE COUNTING METHOD

The most sophisticated method of cycle counting, and the one preferred by most accountants, is to break your inventory up into A-B-C classifications. Items are not treated equally. Based on classification, the A items will be counted more frequently than the B items, and the B items will be counted more frequently than the C items.

The A-B-C method may not be appropriate to your particular business. This approach is based on the items in a particular category actually being part of the active inventory throughout an entire 12-month cycle count period. In other words, if you wish to count the A Category items 12 times per year, they must actually be part of the inventory throughout that year.

If your business is highly seasonal or by its nature features an ever-changing product or item base, then the A-B-C method is not appropriate.

An example of a business where the A-B-C method is probably not appropriate would be a "job shop" manufacturer. Job shops produce an item pursuant to a specific order. Therefore, although the organization will certainly use a number of standard items it always has on hand for that job, many of the things it uses will be obtained for that order alone. These specific items will be purchased, used, and not replaced. They will not be around long enough to be part of an A-B-C count cycle. A method that analyzes items "in the house" at a given point in time would be more appropriate in a job shop environment.

The classifications in the A-B-C method are based on "Pareto's Law"— the 80-20 Rule. See Chapter 3 for a discussion of Pareto's Law and of how to determine which SKUs go into which categories using a single criterion for establishing *value*.

For cycle counting purposes, classifications are determined by "value." Value could be based on money, usage rate, acquisition lead times, the critical nature of an item, or a combination of two or more factors.

Because Chapter 3 deals with item placement, usage rate was used as the value criterion.

There are a number of problems with using a single criterion to establish your A-B-C categories for cycle counting purposes, including:

▶ The criterion used may not be reflective of the entire inventory. For example, if you use dollar value alone, a number of high-dollar items that are infrequently sold or used would become A Category items, while low-dollar items that are used or sold in large quantities would become C Category items.

▸ Different departments in your organization have different and sometimes conflicting interests. For example, individuals charged with balance sheet responsibilities will be concerned with dollar value, while stockkeepers and production managers will be more interested in quantities and usage rates. Purchasing agents will have the additional concerns of acquisition lead times and the criticality ("Just gotta have it when we need it") of various items. By using a single criterion you will almost certainly alienate someone.

Because of the problems associated with using a single criterion to establish A-B-C categories for cycle counting purposes, this author strongly recommends that you use at least two criteria. The technique for blending two (or more) criteria into a single blended value for your analysis is explained below.

Step-By-Step Implementation of the A-B-C Cycle Count Method

You can create a single value from two or more criteria by multiplying the values of one criterion by the values of another criterion. Then you use the blended value for your analysis. Here's how you do it:

▸ Perform Pareto analysis of SKUs utilizing desired criteria. See Chapter 3 and Exhibit 6–8.

▸ Assign SKUs into A-B-C categories. See Exhibit 6–9.

▸ Decide count frequency of each category. See the section, "Determining A-B-C Count Frequency," below.

▸ Multiply respective number of SKUs per category by desired frequency to establish total counts. Cycle is assumed to be one year. See Exhibit 6–10.

▶ Divide total counts by the number of count days (for example, 200 days per year) to determine number of items to be counted each day. See Exhibit 6–10.

▶ Ask yourself, Is this a reasonable number of daily items? If "Yes," proceed. If "No," then change the frequencies and recalculate until a reasonable daily total is established.

▶ Determine how many items from each category will be counted each day. See Exhibit 6–10.

• Divide the number of annual counts within each category by the total (annual) number of counts. This establishes the percentage of counts represented by the respective categories when compared to the total counts.

• Multiply the A, B, and C percent of total by the number of items to be counted daily. This establishes the quantity of each category to be counted each day.

▶ Count each category the desired number of times using the diminishing population technique.

(text continues on page 205)

Exhibit 6–8 Pareto's Analysis Using Two Criteria

1	Column A =	Total number of SKUs (discrete items)
2	Column B =	Item's specific identification number
3	Column C =	Item's description
4	Column D =	Item's unit cost
5	Column E =	Item's annual usage
6	Column F =	Derived from multiplying Column D by Column E. Column F represents the SKU's "blended" usage/cost value
		AFTER STEP 6 — Sort Columns B, C, D, E, and F in descending order, using Column F as the primary sort field. [NOTE: Columns B, C, D, E, and F constitute the sort range. F is the field used to sort the range.] THEN:
7	Column G =	Derived by adding every row of Column F to the sum of all rows above it. This cumulative value column allows for the calculation of a blended percentage value of all items for selected groupings (A-B-C) of items.
8	Column H =	Derived from dividing each row of Column G by the sum (last value in column) of Column G. Column G represents the blended percentage value of all items for selected groupings (A-B-C) of items.
9	Column I =	Percentage of all SKUs represented by a grouping of items. Derived by dividing each row of Column A by the last number of Column A.

(continues)

(Exhibit 6–8 Continued.)

A	B	C	D	E	F	G	H	I
Line No.	Part No.	Description	Unit Cost +	Annual Usage +	Annual Usage Value	Cumulative Usage Value	% Total Value	% Total Items
1	AB103	Item LM	21.60	3,022	65,275.20	65,275.20	3.6%	0.3%
2	ZL8100	Item A	328.00	178	58,384.00	123,659.20	6.9%	0.7%
3	VN-L1079	Item ZK	24.99	1,976	49,380.24	173,039.44	9.7%	1.0%
4	VN-A1267	Item Q	79.99	587	46,954.13	219,993.57	12.3%	1.3%
5	VN-L0572	Item W	8.49	4,899	41,592.51	261,586.08	14.6%	1.7%
6	BCA65100	Item R	2,000.00	19	38,000.00	299,586.08	16.7%	2.0%
7	XL479	Item T	74.00	444	32,856.00	332,442.08	18.6%	2.3%
8	ONV 180	Item PT	36.95	889	32,848.55	365,290.63	20.4%	2.7%
9	VN-A0606	Item VC	17.95	1,666	29,904.70	395,195.33	22.1%	3.0%
10	NV-65525	Item XR	36.40	788	28,683.20	423,878.53	23.7%	3.3%
11	VN-A0604	Item XT	17.49	1,530	26,759.70	450,638.23	25.2%	3.7%
12	AB65771	Item M	42.85	614	26,309.90	476,948.13	26.6%	4.0%
13	SRP-1442	Item S	34.00	765	26,010.00	502,958.13	28.1%	4.3%
14	MND55303	Item QP	25.97	986	25,606.42	528,564.55	29.5%	4.7%
15	ZL427	Item LS	48.00	533	25,584.00	554,148.55	31.0%	5.0%
16	PF5000	Item LC	29.95	843	25,247.85	579,396.40	32.4%	5.3%
17	SRP123	Item IT	12.00	1,888	25,000.00	604,396.40	33.8%	5.7%
75	VN-A1217	Item KL	1.29	5,788	7,466.52	1,424,352.99	79.6%	25.0%
76	LKR-2313	Item KJ	39.75	185	7,353.75	1,431,706.74	80.0%	25.3%
77	VN-N0592	Item GW	34.99	199	6,963.01	1,438,669.75	80.4%	25.7%
78	NF-92251	Item CV	36.40	189	6,879.60	1,445,549.35	80.8%	26.0%
79	VN-F1128	Item BV	126.99	54	6,857.46	1,452,406.81	81.1%	26.3%
80	HWT-3	Item BMM	19.95	325	6,483.75	1,458,890.56	81.5%	26.7%
81	VN-F6405	Item LM	7.49	861	6,448.89	1,465,339.45	81.9%	27.0%
82	L1100-CL	Item SM	1,240.00	5	6,200.00	1,471,539.45	82.2%	27.3%
97	VN9920	Item JB	41.80	98	4,096.40	1,546,606.04	86.4%	32.3%
98	BTL2117	Item CM	5.85	698	4,083.30	1,550,689.34	86.6%	32.7%
99	VN-S3000	Item DB	99.00	41	4,059.00	1,554,748.34	86.9%	33.0%
100	VN-N1433	Item MM	74.99	52	3,899.48	1,558,647.82	87.1%	33.3%
101	VN-A0515	Item NL	17.49	220	3,847.80	1,562,495.62	87.3%	33.7%
102	BTL506202	Item IH	754.00	5	3,770.00	1,566,265.62	87.5%	34.0%
292	VN-F1053	Item KB	1.69	20	33.80	1,789,820.09	100.0%	97.3%
293	VN-B0720	Item RC	3.49	7	24.43	1,789,844.52	100.0%	97.7%
294	MNY764	Item SC	6.72	3	20.16	1,789,864.68	100.0%	98.0%
295	VN-N2606	Item MH	3.99	4	15.96	1,789,880.64	100.0%	98.3%
296	BG321	Item AMH	12.08	1	12.08	1,789,892.72	100.0%	98.7%
297	VN-F1042	Item JB	1.89	5	9.45	1,789,902.17	100.0%	99.0%
298	LFJ-81012	Item BB	13.46	-	-	1,789,902.17	100.0%	99.3%
299	S109	Item AB	8.39	-	-	1,789,902.17	100.0%	99.7%
300	SD20	Item RM	66.65	-	-	1,789,902.17	100.0%	100.0%

Exhibit 6–9 Assigning SKUs into A-B-C Categories

A	B	C	H
Line No.	Part No.	Description	% Total Value
1	AB103	Item LM	3.6%
2	ZL8100	Item A	6.9%
3	VN-L1079	Item ZK	9.7%
4	VN-A1267	Item Q	12.3%
5	VN-L0572	Item W	14.6%
6	BCA65100	Item R	16.7%
7	XL479	Item T	18.6%
8	ONV 180	Item PT	20.4%
9	VN-A0606	Item VC	22.1%
10	NV-65525	Item XR	23.7%
11	VN-A0604	Item XT	25.2%
12	AB65771	Item M	26.6%
13	SRP-1442	Item S	28.1%
14	MND55303	Item QP	29.5%
15	ZL427	Item LS	31.0%
16	PF5000	Item LC	32.4%
17	SRP123	Item IT	33.8%

Category A
Generally made up of those items constituting approximately 75% of the total value of all items.

(continues)

(Exhibit 6–9 Continued.)

A	B	C	H
Line No.	Part No.	Description	% Total Value
75	VN-A1217	Item KL	79.6%
76	LKR-2313	Item KJ	80.0%
77	VN-N0592	Item GW	80.4%
78	NF-92251	Item CV	80.8%
79	VN-F1128	Item BV	81.1%
80	HWT-3	Item BMM	81.5%
81	VN-F6405	Item LM	81.9%
82	L1100-CL	Item SM	82.2%
97	VN9920	Item JB	86.4%
98	BTL2117	Item CM	86.6%
99	VN-S3000	Item DB	86.9%
100	VN-N1433	Item MM	87.1%
101	VN-A0515	Item NL	87.3%
102	BTL506202	Item IH	87.5%
292	VN-F1053	Item KB	100.0%
293	VN-B0720	Item RC	100.0%
294	MNY764	Item SC	100.0%
295	VN-N2606	Item MH	100.0%
296	BG321	Item AMH	100.0%
297	VN-F1042	Item JB	100.0%
298	LFJ-81012	Item BB	100.0%
299	S109	Item AB	100.0%
300	SD20	Item RM	100.0%

Category B
Generally made up of those items constituting from approximately 76% to 80% of the total value of all

Category C
Generally made up of those items constituting from approximately 81% to 100% of the total value of all items.

Exhibit 6–10 Determining How Many Items from Each Category Will Be Counted Each Day

Number of counts per year taken from Exhibit 6–8.

Category	Annual Counts		Total Annual Counts		Percent of All Counts
A	3,300	÷	8,800	=	.375 > 38%
B	2,100	÷	8,800	=	.238 > 24%
C	3,400	÷	8,800	=	.386 > 39%

Category	Total Daily Counts		Percent of All Counts		Number of SKUs to Be Counted Daily
A	3,300	x	38%	=	16.72 > 17 A SKUs per day
B	2,100	x	24%	=	10.56 > 11 B SKUs per day
C	3,400	x	39%	=	17 C SKUs per day

Count each category the desired number of times using the diminishing population technique.

Determining A-B-C Count Frequency

Determine count frequency by:

▶ Deciding count frequency of each category. You can count the respective categories the number of times you desire. There is no rule-of-thumb. You may want to count "A" items 12 times per year, "B" items 4 times per year, and "C" items 2 times per year. See Exhibit 6–8.

▸ Multiplying the respective number of SKUs per category by the desired frequency to establish total counts. Cycle is assumed to be one year. See Exhibit 6–11.

▸ Dividing the total counts by the number of count days (for example, 200 days per year) to determine the number of items to be counted each day.

Determining How Many Items from Each Category Will Be Counted Each Day

It's now time to compute how many items from each category must be counted each counting day to achieve the number of counts for each respective category you desire.

▸ Divide the number of annual counts within each category by the total (annual) number of counts. This establishes the percentage of counts represented by the respective categories when compared to the total counts. See Exhibit 6–10.

Multiply the A, B, and C percent of total by the number of items to be counted daily. This establishes the quantity of each category to be counted each day. See Exhibit 6–10.

WHEN TO COUNT

The ideal time during the day to cycle-count would be when there is no movement of paper or product. You may, therefore, want to count:

▸ At end of business day
▸ Prior to start of day
▸ Over the weekend
▸ During slowest shift

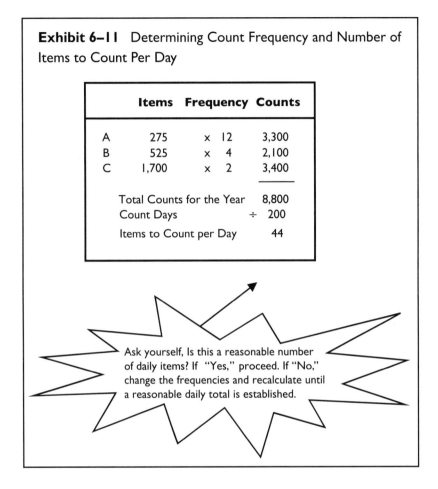

Exhibit 6–11 Determining Count Frequency and Number of Items to Count Per Day

	Items	Frequency	Counts
A	275	x 12	3,300
B	525	x 4	2,100
C	1,700	x 2	3,400

Total Counts for the Year		8,800
Count Days	÷	200
Items to Count per Day		44

Ask yourself, Is this a reasonable number of daily items? If "Yes," proceed. If "No," change the frequencies and recalculate until a reasonable daily total is established.

Another alternative is to creating a cycle counting cut off during a regular business day by using time-of-day.

To use this approach you would:

1. Create a list of items to be cycle-counted the next day.

2. Distribute the list to Shipping, Receiving, the stock put-away workers, order fillers, and data entry clerks.

3. Have Receiving, Shipping, the stock put-away workers, order fillers, and data entry clerks all note the time of day they interacted and actually dealt with any of the items on your list.

4. You now have the ability to audit back into any timeframe during the day. For example:

- You cycle-count widgets at 1:00 PM using a stock status report generated by data entry at 11:30 AM.

- You find that there are 10 less widgets on the shelves than the stock status shows.

- You review all of the paperwork from these different departments.

- The receiving paperwork shows that 10 widgets were received at 10:30 AM.

- There is no paperwork from the stock put-away workers indicating that the widgets were ever moved into stock.

- The missing widgets are sitting out in the dock area. Your record count matches what you have in-house.

WHO SHOULD COUNT

If there are four hours of counting involved in cycle-counting all items on any given day, should you have a single person count for four hours and then begin any necessary reconciliations—or does it make more sense to have four people count for one hour each and then let the inventory control clerk have the rest of the day to correct any problems? It makes sense to spread the raw counting portion of the cycle count among a group of people. This will allow the inventory control clerk to devote more hours of each day to actually fixing the system as opposed to spending each day counting boxes.

R*ecap*

The objective of this chapter was to provide you with insights as to why many inventory control systems fail.

Often failure is due to individuals in different departments simply not understanding the unintended consequences of their own actions.

A review of who is supposed to write something down, what they are supposed to write down, who they are to give the information to, what that person is supposed to do with the information, and the sequencing and overall timing of these events often reveals that respective departments are using different units of measure to define inventory. Some use dollars, while others use actual physical units. In addition, seemingly simple issues like the timing of when an item is entered into the computer system or who is allowed to actually see various items of information can cause severe misunderstandings and inventory inaccuracies.

In analyzing "what is going on," metrics should be used, with the old management phrase, "You can't control what you don't measure," being a constant guiding principle.

By documenting the who, what, when, where, why, and how of how the system is actually working you can demonstrate to yourself and others where changes might be necessary.

REVIEW QUESTIONS

1. Cycle counting is:
   (a) counting a statistically significant cross-section of your inventory frequently.
   (b) counting everything in your facility at least twice per cal-

endar or fiscal year.

(c) determining a fair valuation of your inventory value at least once per fiscal year.

(d) counting all of the bicycle parts in your facility.

2. Flow charts allow you to:

(a) analyze the sequential sequence of a set of events.

(b) determine trends.

(c) compare a projected value against an actual one.

(d) create a report that identifies the number of items per level and number of tiers of product on a flow-through rack.

3. Run charts allow you to:

(a) analyze the sequential sequence of a set of events.

(b) determine trends.

(c) compare a projected value against an actual one.

(d) create a report that identifies the number of items per level and number of tiers of product on a flow-through rack.

4. True or False

The diminishing population method of cycle counting involves counting items when that SKU's stock level reaches zero.

(a) True

(b) False

5. Fill rates indicate:

(a) how much of a particular SKU you have in stock at the end of a calendar month.

(b) the quantitative nature of your inventory.

(c) if you had what you needed when you needed it.

(d) the ratio of accurate shelf counts to record counts.

Answers

1. (a), 2. (a), 3. (b), 4. (b), 5. (c)

Notes

1. *Backflushing* refers to a software technique where raw materials and other components going into a particular subassembly or final product are relieved from stock when that subassembly/product is completed. If there were a seat and a leg assembly that goes into making up a stool, then upon completion of the stool these items would be deleted from inventory. Until the backflush occurs the respective parts, subassemblies, and so on remain in the record count. Contrast this to having each item relieved from stock as it is removed from the shelf for production purposes. Backflushing reduces the time and effort involved in tracking individual inventory transactions.

2. *Work in process* is used to describe raw materials, parts, and subassemblies as they are being used to produce the next higher level component or finished item in a bill of materials (the recipe of materials going into an assembly of some type).

3. *Allocation* refers to an item being tied to a specific order. "Relieving" an item refers to it actually being removed from stock in terms of both its paper life and its real life.

4. It is a rule of thumb that cycle counting should be done 4 days per week, 50 weeks per year, 200 days per year.

CHAPTER 7

BASICS OF SUPPLY CHAIN RISK MANAGEMENT

Supply Chain Management (SCM) is a set of procedures and protocols utilized to integrate suppliers and their suppliers, manufacturers, warehouses, and retail stores to enable merchandise to be produced and distributed with the right quality, in the right quantities, to the right locations, at the right times, in order *to eliminate or minimize system-wide costs, while satisfying service-level requirements.*

Supply Chain Risk Management (SCRM) deals with the risks associated with supply chains that may stretch from Tasmania to Tacoma.

The objective of this chapter is to identify and address some of the significant risks associated with SCM.

SCM in a Perfect World

In a perfect world (which, of course, does not exist), SCM would be the ultimate application of JIT/ERP—one in which all parties would flow inventory to and through one another with no waste. (See Chapter 5.) SCM is the next step beyond JIT/ERP concepts that are employed only within a limited number of transaction participants. It seeks to apply JIT/ERP concepts to the entire supply chain—from end to end.

Stockkeepers, especially in the manufacturing environment, have steadily moved toward SCM. See Exhibit 7–1.

Samuel Slater, popularly known as the "Father of the American Industrial Revolution," or the "Father of the American Factory System," established the first successful American cotton mill at Pawtucket, Rhode Island in 1793. Before the end of the eighteenth century, Eli Whitney, the inventor of the cotton gin, dramatically affected the industrial development of the United States when, in manufacturing muskets for the government, he developed the American mass-production concept of semiskilled workers using patterns, templates, and jigs to produce identical, interchangeable

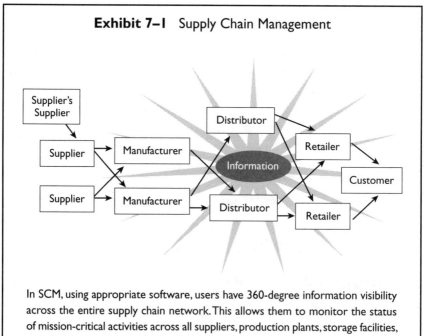

Exhibit 7–1 Supply Chain Management

In SCM, using appropriate software, users have 360-degree information visibility across the entire supply chain network. This allows them to monitor the status of mission-critical activities across all suppliers, production plants, storage facilities, and distribution centers.

parts. Suddenly there was a need to have the right item in the right quantity. Enter risk.

In a perfect world, a manufacturing business buys stuff (raw materials), turns the stuff into something of greater value (the product), and sells it for a higher price. And, it accomplishes all that while only buying and producing the item when the customer wants it. In other words, it always accurately forecasts both requirements and demand. The risks are not receiving what you need when you need it or buying and receiving what you thought you needed, but didn't.

Throughout the Industrial Revolution and for many years after, the lack of transportation, communications, and information management systems limited the amount of coordination and risk reduction achievable among suppliers, manufacturers, distributors, and end users. It was not until the early 1960s, when Joseph Orlicky, an engineer working with IBM, introduced the concept of Materials Requirements Planning (MRP), that some of the risks inherent in an ever-expanding supply chain were first addressed. Conceptually, MRP is a terrific idea. Product demand is linked to raw material supply, and a computer does the calculations, allowing you to only buy what is required at the latest possible opportunity, while ensuring that the customer forecast is met in its entirety. MRP enables you to carry less working and safety stock, resulting in significantly increased profitability. (See Chapter 5.) But it doesn't eliminate risk. By allowing for less safety stock, MRP actually increases risk. This is especially true today as globalization has stretched supply chains around the planet. If natural disasters, political upheaval, or terrorist actions prevent goods from reaching you and you lack sufficient buffer stock to carry you until the next delivery, the negative impacts are obvious.

The advent of JIT/Lean manufacturing systems in the 1980s further increased supply chain risks. With JIT there is no safety stock. There is an increased reliance on single-source suppliers. There is no margin of error for tainted, damaged, or otherwise unsuitable materials. If things go wrong, they go wrong dramatically.

It's not a perfect world.

Primary Risks in SCM

The primary risks associated with SCM are discussed in the following sections.

GLOBALIZATION AND SUPPLY CHAIN COMPLEXITY

Your supply chain runs end-to-end—from point-of-origin to end use. Since there are so many organizations involved, from local concerns to international enterprises, you are only able to exert influence over limited parts of it (unless your organization is extremely large and influential). Therefore, a major risk inherent in most supply chains is simply the lack of control you have over most of the forces driving it.

During the 1920s, organizations attempted to control supply chain risks through vertical integration. In other words, companies tried to control as many aspects of the supply chain as possible "in-house." Organizations tried to control their supply chain risks by carefully locating their facilities in safe locations (away from areas prone to floods) and close to supply points, controlling how their facilities were operated, and carrying larger quantities of safety stock. Basically, this was a "self-contained" approach.

One of the more dramatic examples of this was the production facility at the Ford Motor Company Rouge River plant in Dearborn, Michigan. Raw materials from Ford-owned mines arrived on Ford-owned freighters. Many other raw components came from Ford-owned forests, glassworks, and a rubber plantation in Brazil. Much of this was delivered on Ford-owned rail lines. (It is interesting to note that the modern Ford Motor Company, with a diverse, out-sourced supply chain, had to shut five of its plants when it couldn't get enough parts from its suppliers in Canada because of reinforced security at the borders in the days that followed the 9/11 attack on the World Trade Center.)

When companies began to internationalize in the late 1950s and early 1960s—that is, to serve foreign markets through facilities in those countries—they merely took the self-contained model with them.

Globalization during the 1980s changed much of what had gone before. With globalization, companies sought out the lowest cost materials and labor throughout the planet. This global search for the lowest manufacturing costs coincided with many manufacturing enterprises following the JIT concepts brought to America by Toyota Motor Corporation. They began to embrace just-in-time inventory levels, single-source suppliers, and lean manufacturing techniques that reduced operating redundancies. Sales and distribution facilities were separated (decentralized) from manufacturing facilities and sited so as to serve specific customers, regions, or countries. In-house capabilities and expertise gave way to outsourcing of noncore functions. Just as companies began to operate with lower levels of safety stock, less centralization and control over operations, and less internal versatility, they began to increase their risks to many *single points of failure*.

A single point of failure within a supply chain causes the entire system to stop working. The volcanic ash that prevents airfreight from moving to or from Europe, the Melamine-tainted product from a single-source supplier that provides the item to thousands of distributors around the world, the act of terrorism or change in political dynamics that chokes off supply or causes uncertainty and wild fluctuations in delivery times throughout the supply chain can cause irreparable harm to a company that isn't practicing SCRM.

Although single points of failure are the most dramatic causes of supply chain system failures, a series of relatively small disruptions in a long supply chain can together result in a catastrophic failure as well.

CONFLICTING INTERESTS

Various entities within the supply chain have different, and often conflicting, objectives. For example:

▸ Raw materials and subassembly suppliers want manufacturers to commit to purchasing large quantities, in stable volumes, with flexible delivery dates. Although manufacturers desire long-term commitments from their suppliers with the lowest volume discounts possible and the highest service levels, they are fearful of overcommitting in the face of customer demand fluctuations. Suppliers want stability while manufacturers want flexibility.

▸ Manufacturers want to reduce their acquisition and production costs by engaging in large production runs. However, that set of goals is in direct conflict with the objectives of both warehouses and distribution centers, which is to reduce inventory levels. Making this even worse is that in reducing their levels of inventory on hand, warehouses and distribution centers have to bring in smaller quantities more often, which increases purchasing and transportation costs.

▸ A large end user may want to buy four of a nonstandard pack size that the distributor can only buy in minimum quantities of six. The distributor doesn't want to lose the customer, but has no use for the additional two items. If the end user won't buy them, but the distributor must acquire them (and can't charge the customer for them), they will become dead stock. See Chapter 2 for a discussion of obsolete and dead stock.

SYSTEM FLUCTUATIONS OVER TIME

Even when an organization is using sophisticated forecasting software or when demand is known because of contractual agreements, SCRM must take into consideration changes in demand and costs, such as seasonal fluctuations, trends, back orders, equipment failures, advertising and promotions, and competitors' pricing strategies.

In addition, as a supply chain grows longer and more geographically diverse, delivery lead times, manufacturing yields, natural and human-made disasters, and the like become real areas of concern. For instance, as replenishment lead time from a supplier grows or if the supplier is unreliable, the buyer must have more safety stock on hand to protect itself from stockouts.

Even with the most sophisticated forecasting techniques, forecasts for a specific item or group of items are often incorrect.

EVOLVING RELATIONSHIPS

A supply chain is organic. It grows, expands, and contracts. Relationships evolve and change. Spheres of influence evolve and change.

Establishing a closer relationship with a supplier can lead to more predictability as well as to lower costs and better efficiencies, while an increase in a specific customer's power may cause pressure to change suppliers or the items and quantities being acquired.

PRODUCT COMPLEXITY

The more complex a product is to manufacture, the greater the skill set and mechanisms needed to create it. Fewer suppliers for these items exist and, therefore, there is consolidation into fewer or single sources. And, the more complex it is, the more it costs to create.

Outsourcing the creation of complex items adds more exposure and single points of failure to your supply chain.

INADEQUACY OF INSURANCE

What is your risk of loss? Quite simply, do you know what you are trying to insure?

Your company can be insured against many risks, but the real risk is not recognizing what your risks are. For example, your terms of sale and/or your purchase terms with *each* supplier or customer will determine when title to the goods transfers, and when the risk of loss attaches. See Exhibit 7–2. You must ensure that a cargo insurance policy insures your goods for all transit exposures, both internationally and domestically, and by any conveyance mode.

In addition to freight terms, your supply chain includes other insurable risks, such as storage/warehouse exposure, consolidation exposure, staging exposure, processing exposure, and fulfillment exposure.

Unfortunately, even adequate dollar amounts of insurance coverage cannot protect you from many of the significant negative impacts of supply chain, such as loss of reputation, customers who seek other suppliers, and higher costs of capital in the future.

Insurance should be your last line of defense, not your first.

SUPPLIERS

Reducing the number of suppliers an entity uses is one of the core

Exhibit 7–2 Freight Terms — Free On Board (FOB)

Terms of Sale	Responsibility for Freight Cost and Transit Risk
F.O.B. Destination, freight prepaid	Seller - Pays freight charges Seller - Bears freight charges Seller - Owns goods in transit Seller - Files claims (if any)
F.O.B. Destination, freight collect	Buyer - Pays freight charges Buyer - Bears freight charges Seller - Owns goods in transit Seller - Files claims (if any)
F.O.B. Destination, freight collect and allowed	Buyer - Pays freight charges and deducts from invoice Seller - Bears freight charges Seller - Owns goods in transit Seller - Files claims (if any)
F.O.B. Origin, freight prepaid	Seller - Pays freight charges Seller - Bears freight charges Buyer - Owns goods in transit Buyer - Files claims (if any)
F.O.B. Origin, freight collect	Buyer - Pays freight charges Buyer - Bears freight charges Buyer - Owns goods in transit Buyer - Files claims (if any)
F.O.B. Origin, freight prepaid and charged back	Seller - Pays freight charges and adds to invoice Buyer - Bears freight charges Buyer - Owns goods in transit Buyer - Files claims (if any)
F.O.B. Destination, freight prepaid and charged back	Seller - Pays freight charges and adds to invoice Buyer - Bears freight charges Seller - Owns goods in transit Seller - Files claims (if any)
Special	Buyer - varies Seller - varies (specifications indicated in body of Purchase Order or as an attachment to the Purchase Order)
Pick Up/Will Call	Buyer - Bears freight charges Buyer - Owns goods in transit

ideas behind JIT/Lean manufacturing. To reduce purchasing costs and gain better control over lead times and quality, firms adopting JIT/Lean manufacturing have gone to single-source suppliers or *tiering*. Tiering is where a supplier network is arranged so that the manufacturer deals with a limited number of "main suppliers."

Certainly there are many benefits to single sourcing. See Exhibit 7–3. However, the economic and control benefits of single sourcing must be compared to the increased supply chain risks that arise from a loss of flexibility when a single-source critical item supplier or a small group of suppliers fail in whole or in part.

Even when multisourcing items, there are risks.

If you use two separate suppliers for the same items, but both are in the same foreign country that is known to have large-scale natural disasters, political instability, unreliable legal systems, or significant terrorist attacks on infrastructure (such as transportation or communications systems), then what will cause one to fail will almost certainly dramatically impact the other. The same risks arise in using multiple suppliers that ship through the same carriers, docks, and the like.

There is certainly nothing wrong with seeking low-cost suppliers around the globe. However, you must factor in the attendant risks when outsourcing to low-developed, high-exposure countries.

THE BULLWHIP EFFECT

In unmanaged supply chains, as transactions move back through the supply chain away from the retail customer, demand variability increases, and small changes in consumer demand can result in large fluctuations in orders placed upstream. Eventually, the network experiences very large swings, as each organization in the supply chain seeks to solve the problem from its own perspective. This phenomenon is known as the *bullwhip effect*.

Exhibit 7–3 Comparative Benefits of Single Sourcing
versus Multiple Sourcing

Single Sourcing	Multiple Sourcing
• A larger customer can gain more control over the entire purchasing process (e.g., sourcing, processing, expediting, inspection, billing, and payment terms)	• Reduce risk of item unavailability by having alternative sources of supply
• Can reduce purchasing costs (e.g., the R factor). See Chapter 2.	• Maintain competition
• Better discounts at higher volume purchases	• Stay in touch with the market (e.g., pricing, new products, trends)
• Able to demand better quality	• Avoid complacency (e.g., being taken for granted, poor customer service on the part of a single-source critical item supplier)
• Able to demand changes in packing (which leads to more cost-effective modes of transportation and handling)	
• Priority availability of items when supplier must favor one customer over another if quantities cannot cover all orders	
• Reduction of inventory based on trusted relationship and lead times	
• Better, more timely information	
• Working with suppliers that are both financially and operationally robust (e.g., more than one manufacturing plant for the desired items).	

The following can all contribute to the bullwhip effect:

▶ Overreaction to backlogs

▶ Holding back purchase orders to reduce inventory

▶ Lack of communication up and down the supply chain

▸ No coordination up and down the supply chain

▸ Delay times for information and material flow

▸ Order batching into larger quantities

Order batching occurs in an effort to:

- Reduce ordering costs.

- Take advantage of transportation economics such as full truckload economies.

- Benefit from sales incentives. Promotions often result in forward buying to benefit more from the lower prices.

- Hortage gaming, such as customers ordering more than they need during a period of short supply, hoping that the partial shipments they receive will be sufficient for their real needs.

- Demand forecast inaccuracies by each supply chain participant.

Basically, variability coupled with time delays in the transmission of information up the supply chain and time delays in manufacturing and shipping goods down the supply chain create the bullwhip effect.

DISRUPTION IN COMMUNICATIONS

Information is at the very heart and soul of SCM. Without information, it is impossible to effectively coordinate activities within a supply chain.

Disruptions of communications, whether due to internal or external factors, are a major supply chain risk.

INADEQUATE SOFTWARE

Inadequate information technology (IT) capabilities are a major supply chain risk. Having too much unstructured information is as bad as having too little or no information. Both will prevent you from preventing, mitigating, and reacting to supply chain risks.

Software used in SCM seeks to pull together all of the information required for major components within a supply chain. Its functions include:

• *Planning*	This is the strategic portion of SCM. Strategic level decisions impact the organization on a long-term basis. They deal with such issues as the near- and long-term goals of the entity, the number, and the location and capacity of its facilities—such as offices, warehouses, manufacturing plants, etc.,—or they may deal with if or how the organization will approach the entire supply chain management concept.
• *Sourcing*	Organizations must choose suppliers to deliver the goods and services they need to create their product. It is important to develop a set of pricing, delivery, and payment processes with suppliers and create metrics for monitoring and improving the relationships.
• *Making or Buying*	In manufacturing enterprises, supply chain managers schedule the activities necessary for production, testing, packaging, and preparation for delivery. In distribution, this is the intake of customer orders and acquiring the product necessary for order fulfillment. Forecasting future inventory needs is an essential element of this portion of SCM. See Chapter 5.
• *Delivery*	Delivery involves all of the logistics of coordinating the receipt of orders from customers, developing a network of warehouses, picking carriers to get products to customers, and setting up an invoicing system to receive payments.
• *Return*	Supply chain planners have to create a responsive and flexible network for receiving defective and excess products back from customers or other end users and supporting customers or end users who have problems with delivered products.

Each of the major supply chain steps above is made up of

dozens of specific tasks, many of which have their own specific software. Some SCM software vendors have assembled many of these different chunks of software together under a single roof, but no one package is right for everyone. It is imperative that in selecting a package for your organization you seek out software that reflects the requirements of your particular industry.

SCM software that interfaces your information with other entities is highly dependent on information and data related to your specific organization. That kind of information is found inside enterprise resource planning software. See Chapter 5. It may also be found in legacy systems, such as collections of Excel spreadsheets scattered throughout an organization's departments.

The Internet has provided the platform for a number of software developers to offer "information hubs." See Exhibit 7–4.

Generally, information hubs are Internet-based, private company–hosted software packages with architecture that allows your company to share important information with your suppliers and customers electronically, in real time, thereby enabling them to work faster, smarter, and more cost effectively.

These hosted and managed services are not ERP systems. They are information enablers that takes the processes and information systems that already exist within your organization and makes them available, in real time, to your customers and suppliers via an electronic interface.

You own the data, decide exactly what data is made available, and who is authorized to receive it. Information hubs merely deliver the information.

The real risk to a supply chain with regard to IT isn't so much that appropriate software and hardware isn't available, but that organizations fail to appreciate how much time, money, and effort must be devoted to IT implementation. Implementing effective IT

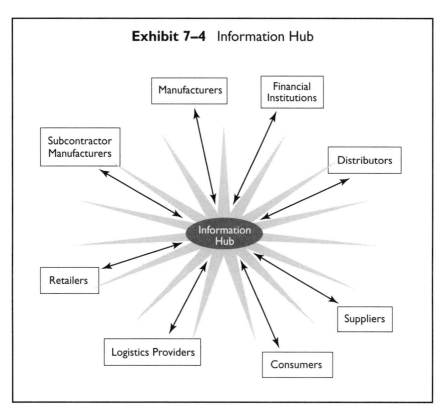

Exhibit 7–4 Information Hub

Manufacturers

Financial Institutions

Subcontractor Manufacturers

Distributors

Information Hub

Retailers

Suppliers

Logistics Providers

Consumers

solutions to supply chain risks always (not sometimes) requires changes in operating processes, changes in corporate culture, and unrelenting, persistent effort.

Suggested Solutions to SCM Problems

The famous quotation by Charles F. Kettering, "A problem well stated is a problem half solved," captures the approach any business must take when undertaking SCRM. To prevent, mitigate, and react to supply chain risks it is essential that you begin by analyzing the risks and determining which must be addressed immediately and in the near term.

ANALYSIS OF RISKS

It is often useful to use charts and graphs to assist you in analyzing supply chain risks.

One approach is to create a Risk and Business Disruption Assessment Chart. See Exhibit 7–5. This approach sets up a spreadsheet. The Assessment can be of the entire supply chain or individual elements within it. For example, you could assess risks associated with each individual supplier, all suppliers within a given geographic area, all suppliers of critical items, your own facilities, etc.

The rows represent risks associated with *natural disasters* (such as earthquakes), *manmade emergencies* (such as strikes and terrorism), and *technological or physical events* (such as a failure of internal or external computer infrastructure or a ship lost at sea).

The columns represent probability, frequency, human impact, property impact, and supply chain impact of the event or occurrence being analyzed.

Exhibit 7–5   Risk and Business Disruption Assessment Chart

Category	Type of Emergency High Low 5 1	Probability High Low 5 1	x	Frequency High Low 5 1	x	Human Impact High Low 5 1	x	Property Impact High Low 5 1	x	Supply Chain Impact High Low 5 1	Total
Natural Disasters											
Manmade											
Technological or Physical											

You then fill in the chart with all of the risks reasonably possible. Do not merely put down the "outlier" events (those that are major but infrequent occurrences). Always include those that are more minor in severity but occur with greater frequency. See Exhibit 7–6.

Exhibit 7–6 Example — Risk and Business Disruption Assessment Chart

Category	Type of Emergency High Low 5 1	Probability High Low 5 1	x	Frequency High Low 5 1	x	Human Impact High Low 5 1	x	Property Impact High Low 5 1	x	Supply Chain Impact High Low 5 1	Total
Natural Disasters											
	Earthquake	4		2		4		5		4	640
	Tsunami	1		1		3		5		2	30
	Volcano eruption	1		1		2		3		2	12
	Hurricane	5		3		2		4		5	600
Manmade											
	Strikes	2		2		2		1		3	24
	Terrorism	2		1		5		5		3	150
	Political instability	1		2		1		1		4	8
	Unreliable legal system	2		1		1		2		3	12
	Bankruptcy–critical supplier	3		1		1		1		5	15
Technological or Physical											
	Commo satellite failure	1		1		1		1		3	3
	Ship lost at sea	5		2		1		3		4	120
	Derailment	3		3		3		1		4	108
	Computer virus	3		2		1		2		5	60

Sortation:

Type Of Emergency	Total
Earthquake	640
Hurricane	600
Terrorism	150
Ship lost at sea	120
Derailment	108
Computer virus	60
Tsunami	30

Type Of Emergency	Total
Strikes	24
Bankruptcy – critical supplier	15
Volcano eruption	12
Unreliable legal system	12
Political instability	8
Commo satellite failure	3

A rating scale is applied to each of the risks identified—for instance, a 1 to 5 scale with 1 as the lowest impact and 5 as the highest. The assessment of values—one to five—is subjective. See Exhibit 7–6.

The rating in each row within a category is multiplied by the value of each preceding column, giving you a numeric total value for the respective events or occurrences. See Exhibit 7–6.

Items are then sorted based on total value in descending order of significance. See Exhibit 7–6. Prioritize which potential disasters can strike your company and prepare for them.

SUPPLIER ASSESSMENT

It is imperative to consider tradeoffs when choosing your approach to using single sourcing versus multisourcing of suppliers.

Consider a hybrid approach. This is where you rely on a main supplier for an item so as to ensure receiving the right item, in the right quantity, at the right place, at the right time, and *at the lowest overall cost*. Then, also establish a relationship with an alternative supplier with more flexible quantities and/or with lower and higher volume limits. The products from this second supplier will be higher; however, you have now increased your flexibility and reduced your supply chain risk.

In addition, consider only using single-source suppliers that have multiple manufacturing facilities for the critical items you are acquiring from them.

Irrespective of whatever sourcing approach used, it is important to assess and select each supplier prudently using a cross-section of criteria. See Exhibit 7–7.

Once you have completed your analysis of potential suppliers and have narrowed down the list to those you truly wish to consider, successful candidates can be selected through a variety of means including competitive bids, reverse auctions,[1] or direct negotiations.

Exhibit 7–7 Supplier Assessment and Audit

Typical areas for review include:

Financial condition	Training
Management	Service programs
Quality assurance controls	Health and safety compliance
Order management	ISO certification(s)
Capacity management	Location of facilities
Engineering capabilities	Political environment
Inspection techniques	Reliability of legal system where supplier is located
Purchasing controls	
Material handling capabilities	Environmental conditions
Claims handling controls	Transportation modalities available

LESSEN THE BULLWHIP EFFECT THROUGH COORDINATION WITHIN THE SUPPLY CHAIN

The solution to the bullwhip effect (where small changes in consumer demand result in large fluctuations in orders placed upstream because of flaws in forecasting supply and demand) is better coordination within the supply chain.

Some major obstacles and solutions[2] to coordination in the supply chain are:

OBSTACLES	SOLUTIONS
Incentive Obstacles	
These are situations in which the incentives offered to different stages or participants in the supply chain result in localized or individual company decisions rather than decisions that reduce variability and overall supply chain costs. It is natural for a stage or participant to maximize those criteria on which it is being rated or incentivized.	• To minimize the effect of incentives on SCM, it is necessary to review the types of decisions employees will make to achieve those incentives. The issue is, Does the incentive lead to decisions that are aligned with the organization's strategic goals? Further, will following the entity's procedures allow the decision maker to achieve the incentive while being in alignment with strategic goals? Basically, are the goals and incentives in alignment or in conflict?
Example: A purchasing manager whose compensation is linked to holding down acquisition costs will buy in larger quantities and generate fewer purchase orders even if that increases inventory carrying costs.	• Any effort to move a sales force from sell-in incentives to sell-through incentives will help reduce forward buying and therefore lessen purchasing fluctuations, and the bullwhip effect.
Example: Manufacturers cannot control the quantities their distributor or retail customers sell. Consequently its sales force isn't incentivized for the quantity sold to the distributor's or retailer's customers (sell-through), but rather the amount they sell to distributor/retailers (sell-in) during some defined period of time (e.g., a month, a quarter). To increase sales during the evaluation period, the sales force will offer whatever price or quantity discounts it controls even if the buyer isn't actually selling the increased quantities. This, in turn, causes unplanned fluctuations in demand. Sell-in incentives create order variability greater than customer demand variability.	One way to move to sell-through is to incentivize the sales force over a rolling time period rather than for sales over a short timeframe (e.g., monthly, quarterly). This lessens the need to push sales hard during one period of time and sell to actual needs during another. Another way to move to sell-through is to incentivize the sales force based on the retailer's sell-through. This, of course, requires that the retailer share relevant point-of-sale information with you.

OBSTACLES	SOLUTIONS
Information Processing Obstacles	
A lack of information sharing between stages of the supply chain will magnify the bullwhip effect where demand information gets distorted as it moves through the supply chain. The result is an increase in variability within the supply chain. Example: In its simplest sense, a retailer will order from its distributor based on orders it receives. In turn, the distributor will order from its supplier based on the orders it receives, and so forth. If one of the parties experiences a one-time spurt in sales, its supplier may incorrectly interpret the increase in orders or order size as a trend, and increase its orders to its supplier, etc. Now assume that a period of random order increases is followed by a period of random decreases. Participants will incorrectly decrease their demand, ultimately causing stockouts and expedited (expensive) purchasing.	• If SCM is to be successful there must be availability of accurate information to each stage of the supply chain. • A key piece of information that should be shared is point-of-sale (POS) data. POS data is important because the objective of any supply chain is to deliver a product to an end user. It is the final customer's order(s) that initiate the need for the supply chain at all. However, each stage of the supply chain uses orders to forecast future demand. Because the needs of different stages vary, forecasts at different stages also vary. If retailers share POS information with other supply chain stages, participants can better forecast future demand, coordinate it with actual end user requirements, and lessen the bullwhip effect. All participants making that effort become more profitable by not buying, making, handling, etc. materials and items that aren't needed at a particular time, if ever. The availability of POS information also allows suppliers, manufacturers, and retailers to engage in collaborative forecasting and planning. Without collaboration, simply having POS information available does very little to improve supply chain performance.

OBSTACLES	SOLUTIONS
Operational Obstacles	
These obstacles include actions taken in placing, taking and fulfilling an order that lead to increased fluctuations in the supply chain. **Example:** To get a better volume discount or to reduce its internal purchasing costs, a customer batches its orders and then purchases six weeks of its needs (a "large lot" order) from manufacturer X. It will not order again for another five to six weeks. In other words, there will be five to six weeks without orders followed by a large order. Another customer does the same thing but places its order with manufacturer X at a different time than the first customer. The manufacturer now has to produce for a demand that is out of sync with actual needs. If the manufacturer, in turn, then batches its orders to its suppliers, the bullwhip effect is magnified. **Example**: Long or erratic lead or order processing times between stages in the supply chain will cause participants to buy and hold larger safety stocks than are justified by actual usage rates. **Example**: A high-demand product is in short supply. The manufacturer wants to ration what it provides to its customers based on the percentage of all orders received. In other words, if it can only fulfill 67% of the total quantity ordered then each customer will receive 67% of its order. Its customers want to game the system by ordering more than they need hoping that the quantity they actually receive will fill all of its customers' orders (e.g., a customer needs 75 of the item but orders 100). Gaming the system leads to inflated needs projections, causing suppliers to build up supplies and capacity for orders that eventually never come.	• One way to stabilize pricing and predictability of supply is to enter into contracts with your suppliers that coordinate activities within the supply chain. Historically contracting for goods and services has been a zero-sum game—I win, you lose. And, if your only objective is to get a one-time, best deal, then there is little incentive to structure agreements so that both sides achieve reasonable objectives. If, however, you want both a good deal and a relationship with a supplier that allows for future "good deals" and better SCM, then you'll have to structure agreements appropriately. Traditional zero-sum contracting does not work in SCM because each party makes decisions independent of the impact of those determinations on other parties.

OBSTACLES	SOLUTIONS
Behavioral Obstacles	
Just as "all politics are local" so, unfortunately, are decisions related to supply chain problems. These problems include: • Each stage of the supply chain approaches issues locally without regard to the impact of its actions up- or downstream from it. • Different stages in the supply chain react to immediate local conditions rather than attempting to identify and correct the root cause(s) of the problem. • Different stages of the supply chain blame one another rather than seeking collaborative solutions. • Because each stage doesn't understand the impact of its actions on another stage, it repeats an action that causes the very problem it's complaining about. • A lack of trust between and among supply chain participants causes them to either not share information or to distrust (and ignore) data provided to them.	By using the techniques above to engage in collaboration with other participants in the supply chain, you and your staff should be able to build trust-based relationships with other participants in the supply chain. As stated earlier in this chapter, any organization that hopes to effectively seize control of its supply chain must commit to a long-term strategic effort.

CONTRACTS THAT DO AND DON'T COORDINATE THE SUPPLY CHAIN

Contracts that coordinate the supply chain are those between supply chain partners that allow every party's objectives to be aligned with the objectives of the entire supply chain.

Wholesale Contracts

The supplier specifies a wholesale price and in return the buyer decides how much to order from the supplier. Specifically, when the retailer places an order, its payment to the supplier is proportional to the quantity it orders.

With wholesale contracts, the retailer generally orders less than the quantity that would be best for the entire supply chain because it bears all the risks of overstocking. Therefore, a wholesale contract does not coordinate the supply chain and, in fact, would tend to make the bullwhip effect more severe.

Buyback Contracts

The supplier specifies a wholesale price and allows the retailer to return unsold inventory up to a specified amount, at an agreed-upon price. This puts some of the risk of overstocking on the seller and leads to a lower price for the buyer.

In these agreements the supplier specifies a wholesale price and a buyback price. For example, a supplier may agree to buy back a $5 item (wholesale price) that has not sold for at least $3 (buyback price). This lowers the loss to the retailer from $5 down to $2. The supplier absorbs the $3 per unsold item as a reduction in margin. The buyback provisions encourage the retailer to buy more product, resulting in more product availability at a higher profit margin for both the supplier and retailer.

A downside to a buyback contract is that it leads to surplus stock that must be disposed of through salvage, return, etc. That, in turn, leads to higher supply chain costs.

Revenue Sharing Contracts

The supplier and the buyer agree on a wholesale price below the typically discounted wholesale price, and in return the supplier receives a fraction of the revenue from each unit sold by the buyer (retailer).

This certainly encourages selling-through as opposed to selling-in as everyone benefits from an increase in product production and sales.

Portfolio Contracts

A number of industrial manufacturers have been outsourcing everything from production and manufacturing to the procurement function itself. The increase in the level of outsourcing implies that the procurement function becomes critical for a manufacturer to remain in control of its destiny. An effective procurement strategy has to focus on both driving costs down and reducing risks.

▶ *Fixed Commitment Contracts*: A traditional procurement strategy that eliminates financial risk is to use fixed commitment contracts. These contracts specify a fixed amount of supply to be delivered at some point in the future; the supplier and purchaser agree on both the price and the quantity to be delivered. The buyer bears no financial risk, but takes huge inventory risks because of uncertainty in demand and the inability to adjust order quantities.

▶ *Option Contracts*: One way to reduce inventory risk is through option contracts in which the buyer prepays a relatively small fraction of the product price up front in return for a commitment from the supplier to reserve capacity up to a certain level.

The initial payment is typically referred to as "reservation price" or "premium." If the buyer does not exercise the option, the initial payment is lost. The buyer can purchase any amount of supply up to the option level by paying an additional price, agreed to at the time the contract is signed, for each unit purchased. This additional price is referred to as "execution price" or "exercise price." The total price (reservation plus execution price) paid by the buyer for each purchased unit is typically higher than the unit price in a fixed commitment contract.

Option contracts provide buyers with flexibility to adjust order quantities depending on realized demand and therefore these contracts reduce inventory risks. These contracts shift risks from the buyer to the supplier since the supplier is now exposed to customer demand uncertainty. This is in contrast to fixed commitment contracts in which the buyer takes all of the risk.

INVENTORY LEVELS

Perhaps the easiest, but certainly not the least expensive, method of reducing supply chain risks is to have more safety stock. It's a tradeoff. More buffer stock, less risk but at a higher cost—less safety stock, more risk of stockouts but at a much lower cost.

Recap

Since the 1980s, companies have wrung costs out of almost every aspect of their businesses. They accomplished this by implementing just-in-time and lean manufacturing techniques and technologies that ruthlessly eliminated or reduced lead times and inventory levels, by utilizing single-source suppliers, and by global outsourcing. The result has been materials and goods making their way to end users through long and complex supply chains.

Only in recent years have organizations begun to truly appreciate and react to the risks inherent in supply chains that have many weak links arising out of uncertain demand and supply, too little information or too much unstructured and therefore unusable information, as well as choke points where a single point of failure can break the entire chain.

REVIEW QUESTIONS

1. "Sell-through" relates to a sales force:
    (a) Selling through deep discounts.
    (b) Selling based on the sales of its customers.
    (c) Selling based on incentives for sales volumes during a defined period of time.
    (d) Selling through strategic alliances.
2. The bullwhip effect refers to:
    (a) The phenomenon where variations in demand fluctuate throughout a supply chain.
    (b) A negotiating tactic in which suppliers must bid against one another for a one-time sale to a retailer.
    (c) The effect on risk in a portfolio contract.
    (d) None of the above.
3. True or False.
    Supply chain management software is unrelated to the information in enterprise resource planning software modules.
    (a) True

(b) False

4. True or False.

Strategic activities deal with getting items into and through an enterprise, while logistical activities deal with suppliers and customers throughout a supply chain.

(a) True

(b) False

5. Information hubs are:

(a) Analyses of all costs associated with initially purchasing an item.

(b) Analyses designed to find the lifetime costs of acquiring, operating, and changing something.

(c) Internet-based, private company–hosted software packages the architecture of which allows a company to share important information with its suppliers and customers electronically.

(d) Both a. and b. above.

Answers

1. (b), 2. (a), 3. (b), 4. (b), 5. (c)

BIBLIOGRAPHY

Anderson, Barbara V. *The Art and Science of Computer Assisted Ordering: Methods for Management.* Westport, Conn.: Quorum Books, 1996.

Arnold, J. R. Tony, and Stephen N. Chapman. *Introduction to Materials Management,* 4th ed. Upper Saddle River, N.J.: Prentice Hall, 2001.

Bernard, Paul. *Integrated Inventory Management.* New York: John Wiley & Sons, 1999.

Bosman, Ruud, *The New Supply Chain Challenge: Risk Management in a Global Economy.* Johnson, RI: FM Global, 2006, retrieved July 15, 2010, from http://www.fmglobal.com/pdfs/Chain Supply.pdf.

Brooks, Roger B., and Larry W. Wilson. *Inventory Record Accuracy: Unleashing the Power of Cycle Counting.* New York: John Wiley & Sons, 1995.

Chopra, Sunil, and Meindl, Peter. *Supply Chain Management: Strategy, Planning and Operation,* 2nd ed. Upper Saddle River, N.J.: Pearson Education, 2003.

Collins, David Jarrett, and Nancy Nasuti Whipple. *Using Bar Coding: Why It's Taking Over,* 2nd ed. Duxbury, Mass.: Data Capture Institute, 1994.

Cullinane, Thomas P., James A. Tompkins, and Jerry D. Smith. *How to Plan and Manage Warehouse Operations,* 2nd ed. Watertown, Mass.: American Management Association, 1994.

Delaney, Patrick R., James R. Adler, Barry J. Epstein, and Michael F. Foran. *GAAP 98: Interpretation and Application of Generally Accepted Accounting Principles 1998.* New York: John Wiley & Sons, 1998.

Eisen, Peter J. *Accounting the Easy Way,* 3d ed. New York: Barron's Educational Series, 1995.

Exforsys, Inc. *Problems with RFID,* n.d. Retrieved April 4, 2010, from http://www.exforsys.com/tutorials/supply-chain/can-rfid-help-your-supply-chain/1.html.

Feld, William M. *Lean Manufacturing: Tools, Techniques, and How to Use Them.* Boca Raton, Fla.: St. Lucie Press/APICS Series on Resource Management, 2001.

Gould, Larry. *What You Need To Know About Supply Chain Management,* n.d. Retrieved July 1, 2010, from http://www.autofieldguide.com/articles/020511.html.

Grieco, Jr., Peter L., Michael W. Gozzo, and C. J. (Chip) Long. *Behind Bars: Bar Coding Principles and Applications.* Palm Beach Gardens, FL: PT Publications, 1989.

Harmon, Craig K., and Russ Adams. *Reading Between the Lines: An Introduction to Bar Code Technology.* Peterborough, N.H.: Helmers Publishing, 1989.

Husdal, Jan. *Supply Chain Management – a complete literature review?, May 29, 2009.* Retrieved July 15, 2010, from http://husdal.com.

IBM Global Services. *The Smarter Supply Chain of the Future,* 2009. Retrieved July 15, 2010, from ibm.com/gbs/supplychainstudy.

InfinityQS. *Mitigating Supply Chain Risk using Collaborative Technology: Trends, Strategies, and a Case Study,* May 2007. Retrieved July 15, 2010, from http://www.infinityqs.com/how-can_supply .html.

Johnston, Michael. *The Information Supply Chain: Data Integrity Rises in Stature.* Raleigh, N.C.: Supply Chain Resource Cooperative, NC State University, 2005. Retrieved August 27, 2010, from http://scm.ncsu.edu/public/security/sec050322.html.

Landvater, Darryl. *World Class Production and Inventory Management.* New York: John Wiley & Sons, 1993.

Leone, Marie. *Inventory: How Fast Is Too Fast?,* August 18, 2005. Retrieved April 5, 2010, from http://www.cfo.com/article.cfm/ 4293058?f=related.

Martinich, Joseph S. *Production and Operations Management: An Applied Modern Approach.* New York: John Wiley & Sons, 1997.

Melnyk, Steven, and R. T. Chris Christensen. *Understanding the Nature of Setups, Part Two: Setups and Lot Sizing* September 9, 2000. APICS Online Edition. www.apics.org/magazine/apr97/basics.htm.

Meredith, Jack R., and Scott M. Shafer. *Operations Management for MBAs.* New York: John Wiley & Sons, 1999.

Palmer, Roger C. *The Bar Code Book: Reading, Printing, Specification, and Application of Bar Code and Other Machine Readable Symbols.* 3rd ed. Peterborough, N.H.: Helmers Publishing, 1995.

Robeson, James F., and William C. Copacino. *The Logistics Handbook.* New York: Free Press, 1994.

Simchi-Levi, David, Edith Simchi-Levi, and Philip Kaminsky. *Designing and Managing the Supply Chain: Concepts, Strategies, and Cases,* 2nd ed. New York: John Wiley & Sons, 2003.

Simchi-Levi, David, Xin Chen, and Julien Bramel. *The Logistics of Logistics: Theory, Algorithms, and Applications for Logistics and Supply Chain Management,* 2nd ed. New York: Springer Science+Business Media, 2005.

Stauffer, David. *Supply Chain Risk: Deal with It.* Boston: Harvard Business School, April 28, 2003. Retrieved July 15, 2010, from http://hbs.edu/item/3442.html.

Supply Chain Resource Cooperative, NC State University. *What is Supply Chain Management?,* n.d. Retrieved August 15, 2010, from http://scm.ncsu.edu/public/basics/.

Technovelgy LLC. *Advantages of RFID Versus Barcodes,* n.d. Retrieved April 4, 2010, from http://www.technovelgy.com/ct/Technology-Article.asp?ArtNum=60.

Technovelgy LLC. *Technical problems with RFID,* n.d. Retrieved April 4, 2010, from http://www.technovelgy.com/ct/Technology-Article.asp?ArtNum=20.

Thomsett, Michael C. *The Little Black Book of Business Math.* New York: AMACOM, 1988.

Thomsett, Michael C. *Winning Numbers: How to Use Business Facts and Figures to Make Your Point and Get Ahead.* New York: AMACOM, 1990.

Tompkins, James A., and Dale Harmelink. *The Distribution Management Handbook.* New York: McGraw-Hill, 1994.

Tompkins, James A. and Jerry D. Smith. *The Warehouse Management Book.* New York: McGraw-Hill, 1988.

Waters, C. D. J. *Inventory Control and Management.* Chichester, West Sussex, England: John Wiley & Sons, 1992.

INDEX